T0316575

Cambridge Elements ≡

Elements in Public and Nonprofit Administration
edited by
Andrew Whitford
University of Georgia
Robert Christensen
Brigham Young University

RETROFITTING COLLABORATION INTO THE NEW PUBLIC MANAGEMENT

Evidence from New Zealand

Elizabeth Eppel
Victoria University of Wellington

Rosemary O'Leary
University of Kansas

CAMBRIDGE
UNIVERSITY PRESS

University Printing House, Cambridge CB2 8BS, United Kingdom

One Liberty Plaza, 20th Floor, New York, NY 10006, USA

477 Williamstown Road, Port Melbourne, VIC 3207, Australia

314–321, 3rd Floor, Plot 3, Splendor Forum, Jasola District Centre,
New Delhi – 110025, India

103 Penang Road, #05–06/07, Visioncrest Commercial, Singapore 238467

Cambridge University Press is part of the University of Cambridge.

It furthers the University's mission by disseminating knowledge in the pursuit of
education, learning, and research at the highest international levels of excellence.

www.cambridge.org
Information on this title: www.cambridge.org/9781108822817
DOI: 10.1017/9781108906357

© Elizabeth Eppel and Rosemary O'Leary 2021

First published 2021

A catalogue record for this publication is available from the British Library.

ISBN 978-1-108-82281-7 Paperback
ISSN 2515-4303 (online)
ISSN 2515-429X (print)

Retrofitting Collaboration into the New Public Management

Evidence from New Zealand

Elements in Public and Nonprofit Administration

DOI: 10.1017/9781108906357
First published online: September 2021

Elizabeth Eppel
Victoria University of Wellington

Rosemary O'Leary
University of Kansas

Author for correspondence: Rosemary O'Leary, oleary@ku.edu

Abstract: This Element is about the challenges of working collaboratively in and with governments in countries with a strong New Public Management (NPM) influence. As the evidence from New Zealand analyzed in this study demonstrates, collaboration – working across organization boundaries and with the public – was not inherently a part of the NPM and was often discouraged or ignored. When the need for collaborative public management approaches became obvious, efforts centered around "retrofitting" collaboration into the NPM, with mixed results. This Element analyzes the impediments and catalysts to collaboration in strong NPM governments and concludes that significant modification of the standard NPM operational model is needed, including the following: alternative institutions for funding, design, delivery, monitoring, and accountability; new performance indicators; incentives and rewards for collaboration; training public servants in collaboration; collaboration champions, guardians, complexity translators, and stewards; and paradoxically, NPM governance processes designed to make collaborative decisions stick.

Keywords: collaboration, new public management, retrofitting collaboration, public administration

ISBNs:9781108822817 (PB), 9781108906357 (OC)
ISSNs:2515-4303 (online), 2515-429X (print)

Contents

1 NPM around the World

This Element is about the challenges of working collaboratively in and with governments in countries with a strong New Public Management (NPM) influence. The NPM is a set of ideas about government reform centered on running government more like a business that peaked in the 1980s and 1990s but is still strong today, albeit in different forms and concentrations, across many countries and jurisdictions. As the evidence from New Zealand used in this Element demonstrates, collaboration – working across organization boundaries and with the public – was not inherently a part of the NPM and was often discouraged or ignored. When the need for collaborative public management approaches became obvious, efforts centered around "retrofitting" collaboration into the NPM, with mixed results. This Element analyzes the varied challenges, successes, and failures that arise when collaborative ideas, approaches, and processes are interjected into New Public Management regimes.

Margaret Thatcher in the UK and Ronald Reagan in the USA are credited with first introducing NPM into their countries, followed by Australia and New Zealand, which developed their own robust variants (Christensen and Lægreid, 2001; Pollitt and Bourckaert, 2017). From the sometimes vague notion of government importing efficient business values and processes (Andrews, 2010) have come several specific cross-cultural themes, including the following (Pollitt and Bouckaert, citing Hood, 1991, 1996; Lane, 2000; Osborne and Gaebler, 1992; and Pollitt, 1990, 2016):

- The prominence of performance and the measure of outputs;
- The creation of lean, flat, small, and specialized or disaggregated organizational forms, and the breakup of larger bureaucracies;
- The extensive use of contracts, not only for procuring government services, but with the heads of public organizations to incentivize and reward performance;
- The use of market-type mechanisms, including competition and pay-for-performance; and
- Referring to and treating the public as customers.

When the NPM was first implemented, many exaggerated its universal acceptance, saying that there was one clear unified direction (Hood 1991, 1995). At its peak, for example, David Osborne and Ted Gaebler, a reporter and a city manager from the USA, published *Reinventing Government* (1992) maintaining that "a similar process is underway throughout the developed world" (1992: 325). Following suit, a junior minister of the UK Treasury said:

> All around the world governments are recognizing the opportunity to improve the quality and effectiveness of the public sector. Privatization, market testing and private finance are being used in almost every developing country. It is not difficult to see why. (Dorrell, 1993)

This exaggeration is attributed to "quick and cheap" rhetoric, as well as data obtained on the Internet "without leaving one's desk" as opposed to sophisticated field research examining the impact of various management practices on government outcomes (Pollitt and Bouckaert, 2017: 13).

In fact, NPM did propagate around the world, but in different forms and strengths. There was a "multiplier effect" where those trained in NPM paradigms trained others, including NPM consultants spreading their gospel when hired by public sector organizations (Pollitt and Bouckaert, 2017: 14). The common themes often were "to restrain public spending, lighten bureaucratic burden, and reshape social policies that can no longer be afforded" (Pollitt and Bouckaert, 2017: 36).

While some scholars summarized NPM as "disaggregation + competition + incentivization" (Dunleavy et al., 2006), others have pointed out that the many streams of NPM make such a standardized view difficult. For example, there are NPM proponents with roots in economics and principle-agent theory (with an emphasis on low trust of public employees [e.g., New Zealand; see Aucoin, 2010]), who wanted to "make the managers manage," and others with roots in leadership and innovation wanting to "let the managers manage" by allowing them leeway to develop creative ways of serving the public. "The hard version emphasize[d] control through measurement, rewards, and punishment, while the soft prioritize[d] customer-orientation and quality, although nevertheless incorporating a shift of control away from service professionals and towards managers" (Pollitt and Bouckaert, 2017: 10).

Today there exists a "shopping basket" of NPM options for reformers (Pollitt, 1995). "[NPM] ... comprises neither a unified theory of, nor a random collection of ideas about, public management. ... [I]t has been applied in different ways with variable effects across a range of jurisdictions, and is thus associated with a varied assortment of policy interventions and reform agendas" (Boston, 2010: 17). Seemingly, a thousand NPM flowers have bloomed across a multitude of jurisdictions – both national and subnational. There are countries – like New Zealand – that ate heartily from the NPM smorgasbord, while there are other countries – like Finland, France, and Japan – that have selectively chosen only a few items to consume from the NPM menu. It should not be surprising, therefore, that NPM results around the world are quite different (Boston et al., 1996; Cheung, 2010; Christensen and Lægreid, 2001; Hansen,

2010; Hood, 1996; Kettl, 2000; Kickert, 2010; Lane, 2000; Pollitt, 1995, 2003, 2016).

One of the strongest themes of NPM concerns performance. The foci here are "performance, results, and efficiency" with an emphasis on "active monitoring" (Pollitt and Bouckaert, 2017: 82–83), and the literature on the topic is vast (Bouckaert and Halligan, 2008; Mayne and Zapico-Goñi, 2017; Mizrahi, 2017; Moynihan, 2008; Talbot, 2010; van Dooren and van de Walle, 2008). The negative spin on performance management is that it created its own bureaucracy to measure, monitor, and judge the performance of NPM organizations and managers. The positive spin on performance is that it has "produced opportunities for citizens to understand better what their governments are producing and this in turn can serve as an impetus to greater public involvement on the output side of government" (Peters, 2010).

After many decades of implementation experiments and "increasing intellectual self-awareness" (Hood and Peters, 2004: 268), the NPM tsunami began to slow around the year 2000 in most countries (Christensen and Lægreid, 2010b; Pollitt and Bouckaert, 2017). Today the strengths, weaknesses, and challenges of NPM have become clearer (see, e.g., Diefenbach, 2009 and Lorenz, 2012), and NPM solutions are no longer necessarily seen as the default setting to address a multitude of public sector challenges. However, NPM is not dead as some have proclaimed (see Dunleavy et al., 2006). "NPM continues to exercise an influence" (Halligan, 2010: 83) and particularly has retained a dominating influence in New Zealand public administration.

Some of the disillusionment concerning NPM comes from the realization that, paradoxically, many anti-hierarchical measures were implemented by ratcheting up hierarchy, calling into question NPM mantras advocating for a break with bureaucracy. Tied in with this was the realization that many anti-bureaucratic NPM reforms have been fostered through the creation of laws that, in fact, created more bureaucracy. Moreover, "making managers manage" may have had the effect of undermining political control (Christensen and Lægreid, 2001:309), with managers subject to public scrutiny and media attention, caught in the middle of the NPM sandwich with politicians on one side and customers on the other. In addition, increased contracting out – a pivot point of NPM (see Pallesen, 2010) – has exacerbated coordination problems in bureaucracies (Kettl, 2016).

Complicating NPM challenges is the fact that objective evaluation of NPM efforts has been patchy at best, with some maintaining that the best governments can do may be to strive for changed organizational culture "talk" and to strive for openness to new ways of managing public programs (Pollitt, 2002). This seemingly simple way forward is, in fact, quite complex, as country and organizational cultures are the water in which NPM swims, often changing the nature of reforms (Byrkjeflot, 2010; Verhoest, 2010). "The NPM … use[d] an overly rational and rather unrealistic set of assumptions.... It also tend[ed] to focus on the inner workings of individual organizations (see, e.g., Brunsson, 2010) and pay less attention to the 'big picture'.... " (Pollitt and Bouckaert, 2017: 214).

In addition, many jurisdictions today have an increased realization of the importance of collaboration, also called joined-up governance, and whole-of-government approaches (Christensen and Lægreid, 2010a; O'Leary, Gerard, and Bingham, 2006; Osborne, Radnor, and Nasi, 2013). Included in this is the idea that the purpose of the public sector is service delivery, which includes the need for customer-centric and codesign approaches (Bingham, Nabatchi, and O'Leary, 2005; Osborne 2010; Osborne, Radnor, and Nasi, 2013). To some, "the horizontal challenge [is now seen] … as even more important than the vertical, because [of] the large number of sectoral pillars or 'silos' created [through NPM]" (Christensen and Lægreid, 2010a). Still, NPM persisted despite the realization that it often failed to address complexity (Diefenbach, 2009), with most efforts to address NPM silo effects added onto NPM programs rather than replacing them (Christensen and Lægreid, 2011; Christensen and Lægreid, 2012, 2015; Lodge and Gill, 2011; Xialong and Christensen, 2019).

Research in the last decade concludes that it is possible to have a strong emphasis on performance while grappling with intraorganizational challenges. In other words, performance and collaboration need not be mutually exclusive. Some researchers, for example, found that collaborative processes, in fact, have been related to better performance (Thomson, Perry, and Miller, 2008). Others have concluded that a balance of intraorganizational foci and interorganizational foci is needed for effective performance governance systems (Halligan, Sarrico, and Rhodes, 2012). An analysis of 1,875 senior leaders in the public and nonprofit sectors found a perceived positive link between collaboration and performance as the main catalyst for engaging in collaboration as a management strategy (Mitchell, O'Leary, and Gerard, 2015). Researchers who examined the interaction of performance and collaboration, both within agencies and across agencies, concluded that extensive investment in individual agency performance systems weakens interagency collaborative performance efforts. "As managers feel as if they will be held accountable to [individual] agency priority goals, they do not become any more likely to collaborate to improve cross-agency priority goals" (Choi and Moynihan, 2019: 1551). In fact, interagency performance goals may undermine interagency collaboration.

1.1 The New Zealand Context

New Zealand's wholesale, root and branch, public management reforms enacted through the Public Finance Act of 1987, the State Sector Act of 1988, and the State-Owned Enterprises Act of 1988 have been well documented internationally and have persisted (with minor tinkering) for thirty years (Aucoin, 1990; Boston, 1991; Boston and Eichbaum, 2007; Pollitt and Bouckaert, 2017; Scott, 2001; Treasury, 1984; Treasury, 1987). The reforms also removed many of the previous centralized public administration directives allowing managers to manage in the most efficient way to deliver their outputs. In essence, the reforms created new, more narrowly focused, public sector organizations in lieu of multifunction departments reporting to a minister through a permanent head. The legislation and accompanying administrative instruments put in place a system of governance and financial management controls seen as typical of NPM (Peters and Savoie, 1998). As Osborne and Gaebler put it, New Zealand went "the farthest along the entrepreneurial path ... [i]n one fell swoop" (1998: 330). See Box 1.

BOX 1 A CLOSE-UP LOOK AT NEW PUBLIC MANAGEMENT CHANGES IN NEW ZEALAND

Examples of NPM changes made in New Zealand may easily be found in the social sector, specifically the Department of Social Welfare, the Department of Education, and the Department of Health. Under NPM, these mega-departments ceased being responsible for the direct delivery of public services such as pensions, unemployment and housing support, education, and health services. The departments instead were separated into policy and service delivery branches, and their services were broken up into measurable units to be contracted out. This had a dramatic effect on the connectedness and coherence of government-funded social services (Boston et al., 1991).

In the education sector, the Ministry of Education was limited to policy development, while operational agencies were formed to provide support to schools and early childhood services, including an agency to provide special education services to children with special needs. Schools and tertiary education institutions acquired their own elected boards and a certain amount of autonomy about their delivery within nationally specified guidelines. There was little or no attention to how issues that cut across these "silos" would be addressed.

Outside of central government, a plethora of statutory authorities such as boards responsible for services like pest control or water quality in a district were swept away and replaced by a single layer of local government bodies responsible for a narrower range of functions in their local area. District councils, elected by people living in their area, are now responsible for local services such as drainage, roads, and garbage. Many of these also provide additional public services such as parks and libraries. Regional councils are responsible for public transportation and environmental management plans as well as environmental monitoring. In some cases, these two types of local government bodies have been merged into large unitary councils performing all these functions, as is the case with the Auckland City Council.

Notwithstanding the local level of government, New Zealand's governance of many social and economic policy areas also is highly centralized. At the national level, departments or ministries are responsible for providing one or more portfolio ministers with policy advice and other specified services. Control tools established under NPM included public service organizations headed by chief executives on fixed-term contracts, as well as annual purchase agreements between the minister and a department that specified the requirements for delivery in terms of outputs. Outputs were constructed from the unbundling of services into discrete specific and measurable deliverables.

The arrangements put in place for accountability and financial management resulted in complex government services being broken down into discrete parts that often became the responsibility of more than one delivery agent. For example, interventions to help at-risk youth find employment might consist of a series of discrete tasks (e.g., delivery of policy advice, interviewing and screening at-risk youth, providing employment readiness training, matching youth and employers) spread across separate agencies. What each agency was responsible for was reduced to a list of tasks or items that could be measured, while the outcome of improving the situation for at-risk youth went unmeasured and unmonitored.

This managerialist frame (as it was named by Pollitt, 1993) became the cornerstone of NPM in New Zealand: Ministers were responsible for policy, and their departments were responsible for implementation and operational matters. Departments were given more freedom to manage through the elimination of many managerial guidelines and restrictions. Many discrete services that could be sufficiently specified were outsourced to third parties – some governmental, some nongovernmental (NGO), some not-for-profit, and some private organizations.

While connecting the cause and effect of NPM reform mantras with actual change can be difficult (Pollitt and Bouckaert, 2017), a prominent New Zealand scholar, Jonathan Boston, summarized the specific goals of reforms in New Zealand as follows, helping us to understand what was intended when major NPM changes swept that country in the 1980s and 1990s. Boston notes that not all the goals received equal weight:

- Improving allocative and productive efficiency, and enhancing the effectiveness of government services;
- Improving both managerial and political accountability;
- Reducing the level of government expenditure and the size of the core public sector;
- Reducing the range of state functions under direct ministerial control, and minimizing opportunities for the non-transparent use of public power;
- Minimizing the risk of bureaucratic, provider or regulatory capture;
- Improving the quality of the goods and services produced by public agencies; and
- Making public services more accessible and responsive to consumers, as well as more culturally sensitive (Boston, 2012: 7).

By most accounts, New Zealand was successful in increasing efficiency and effectiveness in large part through the never-ending efforts of the Ministry of Finance and the State Services Commission (Boston et al., 1996), creating the vertically streamlined government it wanted. These agencies were zealous in their oversight of the administrative side of the reforms in individual departments and agencies to ensure that there was no slipping back into what was seen as the pre-reform culture in which costs tended to escalate and accountabilities tended to blur because the policy and delivery arms of government were interlinked, and service providers were "captured" by the sectors they administered. Chief executives were held accountable for the delivery of their department's programs, on time and within budget.

Tenure of employees was dramatically lessened, with all members of the New Zealand Senior Executive Service mandated to reapply for their jobs after five years. Chief executives, whose tenure was governed by contract, could serve for a maximum of eight years (five years plus three after favorable review of performance). Promotion was tied to the accomplishment of specific goals rather than conferred by seniority. Annual pay increases of civil servants and the centralized negotiation of non-pay conditions of public employees were abolished. The civil service was brought under the Labor Relations Act that previously applied only to the private sector. In short, the civil service deliberately became "deprivileged" (Pollitt and Bouckaert, 2017: 94).

At the same time, several of the NPM goals received little or no attention (Boston, 2012; Schick, 1996; Scott, 2001), including the following:

- Developing new forms of governance for the handling of complex and controversial policy issues, such as joined-up governance, collaborative governance and co-management;
- Enhancing horizontal coordination across governmental organizations and more joined-up service delivery; and
- Increasing the role of citizens, as opposed to consumers, customers and clients, in the design, delivery, oversight and control of public services (Boston, 2012: 8).

Hence, although NPM was often presented as focused on outcomes, the reality of the reform fell far short of its intentions. In fact, its implementation reinforced organizational and service silos (sometimes called stovepipes) that impeded outcomes. As a result, any initiative requiring collaboration, joined-up approaches, or citizen participation became more difficult to achieve.

One of the biggest problems turned out to be the design principle behind some of the reforms that "all state organizations should, at least ideally, have only one main function" (Boston, 2012: 8). This led to the decoupling of programs and institutional fragmentation that hinders outcome achievement today. Tied in with this, there have been unanticipated consequences of the NPM reforms that serve as impediments to, and inhibitors of, collaboration, which we explore in this Element.

New Zealand may have focused too heavily on accountability at the expense of personal responsibility – a phenomenon that inhibits collaboration, concluded a public finance expert:

> [T]he words [responsibility and accountability] lead down very different managerial paths. Responsibility is a personal quality that comes from one's professional ethic, a commitment to do one's best, a sense of public service. Accountability is an impersonal quality, dependent more on contractual duties and information flows. Ideally, a manager should act responsibly, even when accountability does not come into play. As much as one might wish for an amalgam of the two worlds, the relentless pursuit of accountability can exact a price in the shrinkage of a sense of responsibility. Responsibility itself is not sufficient assurance of effective performance; if it were, there might have been no need to overhaul public management. Yet something may be lost when responsibility is reduced to a set of contract-like documents and auditable statements. (Schick, 1996: 84–85)

New Zealand fell for NPM and fell hard. It is considered one of the strongest creators, proponents, developers, and implementers of NPM in the world, striving to be what Pollitt and Bouckaert (2017: 158) call a "high-change country." As NPM reforms receded in other countries that often developed a growing appreciation for, and an interest in, collaboration, joined-up governance, and whole-of-government approaches (Christensen and Lægreid, 2010b; Osborne, Radnor, and Nasi, 2013), the ghost of NPM past has remained in New Zealand, making collaborative public management and working across boundaries difficult, as this Element demonstrates.

There have been efforts to plug these NPM holes in New Zealand with programs that have been added on to – and have not replaced – NPM. Most notably, an early attempt was the naming of Strategic Results Areas, as well as Key Results Areas, that strived for cross-organization collaboration (Boston et al., 1996: 282–283). The Better Public Services program pursued from 2011 to 2016 established a renewed focus on targets aimed at achieving results for New Zealanders as a whole.

The Performance Improvement Framework (PIF) was added to NPM performance efforts in 2009 to help top managers in New Zealand government lead performance improvement in their agencies and across the system over a four-year time horizon. Yet researchers who analyzed the PIF in 2019 found "problems emanating from the continuing influence of NPM" with NPM-style performance measurements "anchor[ing] the process in a backwards looking view of performance against static expectations. . . . demonstrating the issues associated with holding on tightly to NPM while significant change occurs" (Allen and Eppel, 2019: 2).

The enduring strong influence of NPM-created organizational silos and administrative machinery in limiting collaboration across boundaries to connect services to meet more complex and evolving needs is perhaps the best reason for the use of data from New Zealand for this Element, coupled with our strong familiarity with New Zealand public administration. One author is a seasoned New Zealand "insider" public servant and scholar who has experienced first-hand, and written about, collaboration challenges in New Zealand for over three decades. The other author is a seasoned U.S. academic who studied the challenges of retrofitting collaboration into NPM in New Zealand as an "outsider" working with the New Zealand government as an Ian Axford Public Policy scholar in 2014 and in subsequent work. By examining how the strong strains of NPM so clearly evident in New Zealand have affected two decades of collaborative efforts, our goal is to develop generalizable understandings and recommendations for other countries seeking to retrofit collaboration ideas, approaches, and processes into their NPM structures and processes.

Toward that goal, this Element is organized as follows:

Section 2 provides a brief overview of theories of collaboration. We examine why and under what circumstances collaboration is essential for the work of government through the theoretical lenses of resource dependency, common purpose, shared beliefs, political interests, and catalytic actors. We also introduce the idea of collaborative leadership. One of the lessons of this section is that there are many diverse reasons why organizations may want or need to collaborate. Another lesson is that collaborative leadership requires both a different mindset and a different skill set than traditional leadership.

Section 3 introduces the culture of the NPM that remains in New Zealand today and has made collaboration difficult and at times impossible. Fear of, and punishment for, collaboration that does not comport with standard operating procedure is prevalent. At times, this fear and punishment have pushed collaboration initiated by New Zealand public servants looking for better ways to serve the public under the radar. The specter of NPM lives on in New Zealand and affects change efforts. At the same time, there is a need for bottom-up creativity, permission to try new collaborative approaches, and the empowerment of those who initiate collaborative approaches.

Section 4 presents three case studies in which collaboration has risen above the radar successfully by adapting the NPM governance system. But abrasion points remain. Two of the case studies – Whānau Ora, designed by Māori to serve Māori, and the Better Public Services (BPS) justice system result areas – are national initiatives. The Southern Initiative, which addresses challenges in a lower socioeconomic part of Auckland that has experienced significant social and economic challenges over many years, is the work of one large local unit, the Auckland City Council.

Section 5 dives into the work of the New Zealand Land and Water Forum and the Canterbury Water Management Strategy, two examples where collaboration was an explicit feature of the governance processes adopted. The Land and Water Forum, a nongovernmental entity, brings together a range of industry groups, environmental and recreational NGOs, iwi (Māori), scientists, and other organizations with a stake in freshwater and land management to discuss, innovate, and collaborate with the goal of developing a shared vision and a common way forward among all those with an interest in water. The analysis in this section highlights tensions with the Forum and the New Zealand government, as well as the roles of law, leadership, and culture in both promoting and slowing collaborative efforts to protect water. Juxtaposed to the Land and Water Forum is the Canterbury Water Management Strategy with local catchment zone committees and a forum of district mayors that has been successful in catalyzing collaboration at the local government level. The strengths and weaknesses of the Canterbury approach are analyzed.

In Section 6 we review the lessons learned from our research and the work of others concerning the uneasy coexistence of collaboration and NPM. Our findings and the work that supports them lead us to identify numerous suggestions for retrofitting collaboration into strong NPM governments. New Zealand, having trodden the path of non-legislated, retrofitted collaboration for two decades, has most recently decided to amend its primary NPM legislation to better catalyze collaboration in New Zealand. We examine what this legislation, passed in late 2020, does and why. It is our hope that our findings and analyses will be useful to other governments strongly imbued with elements of NPM.

2 Collaboration as a Public Management Tool

Before we dive into examining the challenges of retrofitting collaborative ideas, approaches, and processes into countries with NPM ideologies, it is important to clarify what we mean by collaboration. Today the term "collaboration" is widely used in all sectors around the world – public, private, and nonprofit. For the purposes of this Element, we define collaboration as the process of facilitating and operating in multi-organizational arrangements to solve problems that cannot be solved or easily solved by single organizations (Agranoff and McGuire, 2003a) and add that collaboration can include the public (O'Leary, Bingham, and Gerard, 2006). Collaboration, as asserted by Gray (1989: 5), "is not really a new concept." Collaboration has been used as a means of accomplishing complex tasks and goals for years. In this work, we focus on the use of collaboration as a public management tool.

As aptly stated by Vangen and Huxham (2012: 731), "[c]ollaboration is a recognized feature of public administration because it provides the means to seek synergistic gains known as collaborative advantage." According to Huxham (1993: 603), a "collaborative advantage will be achieved when something unusually creative is produced – perhaps an objective is met – that no organization could have produced on its own and when each organization, through the collaboration, is able to achieve its own objectives better than it could alone. In some cases, it should also be possible to achieve some higher-level ... objectives for society as a whole rather than just for the participating organizations." Here, we explore some of the reasons for the use of collaboration in the context of public management.

2.1 Theoretical Reasons for Collaboration

On the theoretical side, there are many explanations as to why public and nonprofit organizations collaborate (O'Leary and Vij, 2012), despite the fact that most scholars of interorganizational collaboration agree that organizations prefer autonomy to dependence (Bryson, Crosby, and Stone, 2006; Hudson, Hardy, Henwood, and Winstow, 1999; Rogers and Whetten, 1982). "Resource dependency" is the most well-developed theory of interorganizational partnership. The basic assumption of resource dependency theory is that individual organizations do not have all the resources they need to achieve their goals and, thus, must acquire resources, such as money, people, support services, technological knowledge, and other inputs to survive (Pfeffer and Salancik, 1978). That is, organizations must rely on a variety of inputs from the collection of interacting organizations, groups, and persons in the external environment (Gazley and Brudney, 2007; Sowa, 2009; Van de Ven, Emmett, and Koening, 1975).

As a consequence of resource-dependent activities, exchange relationships develop. Levine and White (1961, 588) define organizational exchange as "any voluntary activity between two or more organizations which has consequences, actual or anticipated, for the realization of their respective goals or objectives." More than just a way to acquire needed resources, interactions based on exchange are "a stabilizing force in the life space of organizations" (Alter and Hage 1993: 45). Exchange relationships stabilize interorganizational linkages by reducing uncertainty about the future provision of resources (see, for example, Galaskiewicz, 1985) and by maintaining consistent interaction patterns (Kickert, Klijn, and Koppenjan, 1997).

Although resource exchange theory is based on the notion of dependency, even relatively independent organizations may collaborate to take advantage of available resources (Ansell and Gash, 2008; Berry, Krutz, Langer, and Budetti, 2008; Emerson, Nabatchi, and Balogh, 2012; Foster and Meinhard, 2002; Gazley and Brudney, 2007; Graddy and Chen, 2006, 2009; Gray, 1989; Pfeffer and Salancik, 1978; Sowa, 2008; Wood and Gray, 1991). Organizations may actively seek out funds within existing network structures, for example, or seek to initiate collaboration to tap into funding sources (Agranoff and McGuire, 2003a; Alter and Hage, 1993).

A second theoretical explanation as to why organization leaders collaborate is "common purpose." Organizations form network linkages to achieve similar, compatible, or congruous goals (Gray, 1989; Rogers and Whetten, 1982). Issues that were previously thought of as single-agency issues are now increasingly understood to have broad linkages and to be interconnected with other issues (Bryson, Crosby, and Stone, 2006; O'Leary, Gerard, and Bingham, 2006). Accordingly, many groups or organizations have partial responsibility to address public challenges (Crosby and Bryson, 2005) and are using collaboration to do so.

Related to common purpose is the notion of "shared beliefs." A similarity in values and attitudes make the formation of interorganizational linkages more probable (Aldrich, 1979; Alter and Hage, 1993) and make these linkages more stable over time (Van de Ven et al., 1975). A common "belief system," including norms, values, perceptions, and worldviews, provides "the principal 'glue' to hold together networks of actors" (Fleishman, 2009; Sabatier and Jenkins-Smith, 1993: 27).

A third theoretical reason for collaboration is its use by organizations to further their "political interests" (Gazley and Brudney, 2007; Heclo, 1978; Kickert et al., 1997; Sabatier and Jenkins-Smith, 1993; Sowa, 2008). Through participation in a policy network, for example, organizations may promote the views or desires of their members or constituencies; gain access to political officials or decision processes and cultivate political alliances; gain political legitimacy or authority; and promote organizational policies or programs.

"Catalytic actors," or leadership both within the organization and by network leaders or coordinators, provide still another theoretical explanation for the formation of collaborative linkages (Agranoff and McGuire, 2001; Bardach, 1998; Kickert et al., 1997; O'Leary, Choi, and Gerard, 2012). Here, individuals acting as leaders or catalysts may provide incentives for organizations to collaborate (Emerson, Nabatchi, and Balogh, 2012). Sometimes this takes the form of an individual whose sense of what it means to be a highly professional actor includes the imperative to collaborate (McGuire, 2009). Other times, the catalytic actor may be an individual who naturally engages in networking throughout his or her career (Hicklin, O'Toole, Meier, and Robinson, 2009).

2.2 Practical Reasons for Collaboration

On the practical side, most public policy challenges extend beyond traditional agency boundaries and require a multiagency approach. Think of any major public policy challenge: housing, poverty, economic inequality, education, pollution, transportation, health care, energy, or many others. To address any one of these challenges effectively, a full-court press is needed with collaboration across boundaries (O'Leary, Gerard, and Bingham, 2006). Furthermore, Johnston et al. (2011: 699) explain, "when successful, a collaborative governance approach can lead to increased government accountability, greater civic engagement, consistent downstream implementation, and most importantly, higher levels of process and program success."

For example, although achieving accountability in the collaborative context presents numerous challenges (Kettl, 2006), the use of collaboration may allow public managers to innovatively solve public problems and therefore respond to the demands of citizens and elected officials (Page, 2004). Second, the use of collaboration can increase citizen involvement and engagement. Bingham, Nabatchi, and O'Leary (2005: 553) argue that new forms of governance such as collaborative governance arrangements may "enhance the individual exercise of voice [and] empower citizens and stakeholders in ways that are different from traditional governance processes." Similarly, citizens often seek additional avenues for engaging in governance, which can result in new and different forms of collaborative problem-solving and decision-making (Bingham, Nabatchi, and O'Leary, 2005; Nabatchi, Gastil, Weiksner, and Leighninger, 2012; O'Leary, Gerard, and Bingham, 2006). As explained by Vigoda (2002: 529),

> [C]ollaboration is an indispensable part of democracy. It means partnership in which authorities and state administrators accept the role of leaders who need to run citizen's lives better – not because they are more powerful or superior, but because this is a mission to which they are obligated.

Regarding policy implementation, successful collaborations may result in future opportunities for more collaboration, changes in norms and practices, and the production of public value (Bryson, Crosby, and Stone, 2006). Finally, public managers use collaboration in an attempt to increase the effectiveness and success of policies and public service delivery (Agranoff and McGuire, 2001; Bingham and O'Leary, 2008; Goldsmith and Kettl, 2009; O'Leary and Bingham, 2007).

2.3 The Challenges of Collaboration

Challenges often arise in collaborations due to "differing aims and expectations that partners bring to a collaboration, tensions in loyalties to home organizations versus the collaboration, differing views about strategies and tactics, as well as from attempts to protect or magnify partner control over the collaboration's work or outcomes" (Bryson, Crosby and Stone, 2015). Sometimes the origin of challenges can be as simple as differing definitions of collaboration or no definition at all. O'Leary, for example, documented hundreds of instances of the terms collaboration, collaborate, collaborative, co-produce, and co-production used by the New Zealand State Services Commission without definition (2014: 34–40).

Other scholars have focused on the competing institutional logics that exist within collaborative organizational forms (Bryson, Crosby, and Stone, 2006). "Institutional logics are sets of rules, symbols, and patterns of action that coalesce around distinguishable institutions and that serve to organize and provide meaning to behavior" (Chiarello, 2015: 93). Participants in collaborations often must respond to competing institutional logics – those that arise out of their home organizations and those that arise out of the collaborations.

Still other scholars have focused on the challenges that emerge specifically for collaborative networks. Collaborative networks can be defined as "collections of government agencies, nonprofits, and for-profits that work together to provide a public good, service, or "value" when a single public agency is unable to create the good or service on its own and/or when the private sector is unable or unwilling to provide the good or services in the desired quantities" (Isett, et al. 2011: i158). Because networks are, by definition, complex organizational forms, the challenges of collaborative networks are numerous. In the context of government, bureaucratic rules, practices, and procedures "impose[] constraints (e.g., competing statutory objectives, conflicting values or missions, budgetary responsibilities, resource constraints, or turf) that limit practitioners' abilities to exploit an interorganizational network's collaborative capacity" (Imperial, 2005: 283). For an overview of the most common challenges, as identified by O'Leary and Bingham (2007), see Table 1.

In addition, there are specific challenges often faced by public managers who collaborate. Borrowing from Connelly, Zhang, and Faerman (2008), here are some paradoxes of being a collaborative manager. While we focus on networks, these challenges pertain also to collaborations outside of networks.

Collaborative managers must work with both autonomy and interdependence. As a leader of a single unit, managers often work autonomously, setting the rules and making decisions independently. As a member of a collaborative network, however, a manager is now one of many, with numerous intertwining interests that must be met.

Collaborative managers and their networks have both common and diverse goals. Each member of a network has goals that are unique to that member's organization or program. At the same time, as members of a network, managers share common goals.

Collaborative managers must work with both a lesser and a greater variety of groups that are increasingly diverse. When organizations combine to form a network, they become one body – hence the smaller number. Yet within this one body is a variety of organizations with different cultures, missions, and ways of operating – hence the greater diversity.

Collaborative managers need to see the forest and the trees. A manager of a single program or organization must master the details and fine points of what they do daily. As a member of a network, that same manager needs to think holistically and laterally. They are working from both ends of the bungee cord – up close with fine-grained detail of how things work on the ground, to up high where a more wide-angle helicopter overview is possible. In this way, they test each action and decision for its effects on the whole.

Collaborative managers need to balance advocacy and inquiry. Every manager has an obligation to promote, support, and act in favor of his or her organization. Yet because of the intertwining interests, managers need to gather the information for decisions necessary to act in the best interests of the

Table 1 The challenges of collaboration

Definition	Explanation
There are multiple members	Each member brings his or her own interests that must be met. If interests are not met, members may leave.
Members bring both different and common missions.	There must be some commonality of purpose to provide incentive for becoming a member. Yet each organization also has its own unique mission that must be followed. These missions can at times clash with the mission of the collaborative.
Organizations have different organizational cultures.	Culture is to the organization what character and personality are to the individual. Just as each individual is unique, so is each organization culture. Diversity among organizations' cultures may present conflict management challenges within the collaborative.
Organizations have different methods of operation.	Collaborating organizations will differ in degrees of hierarchy. They will differ in degrees of management control. These and other differences may affect what a collaborative can and cannot accomplish and the speed at which it is accomplished.
Members have different stakeholder groups and different funders.	To satisfy their diverse constituencies, members will have different perspectives on appropriate direction and activities. Some of these preferences will overlap, some will not.
There are often multiple issues.	Collaboratives typically are formed to address complex problems that may have contested explanations of their origins and perceived solutions and are not easily solved by one organization. Complex problems bring with them multiple issues and sub-issues. Multiple issues and sub-issues typically yield multiple challenges needing conflict management.

There are multiple forums for decision-making.	Public decisions may be made by collaboratives. At the same time, the same public issue may be debated and dealt with in the legislature, in the courts, or in the offices of career public servants. Whether and how a decision is made by a collaborative can be a source of conflict. Multiple forums also may make it difficult to keep organizations committed to collaborative solutions.
Collaboratives are both interorganizational and interpersonal.	Networks typically are spider webs of organizations. But each organization typically is represented in the collaborative by one or more agents of that organization. Just as collaborating organizations may clash, so too may individuals.
There is a variety of governance structures available.	How the collaborative chooses to govern itself, lead members, develop consensus, and create conventions for dialogue and deliberative processes are all exceedingly important and demanding. Just the design of governance rules can be a complex procedure.
Collaboratives may encounter conflict with the public.	Increasingly, collaborative public management arrangements are engaging citizens through a variety of means. Because collaboratives often address issues of concern to the public, conflict may emerge.

Adapted from O'Leary and Bingham, 2007

network. What is a manager to do? Connelly, Zhang, and Faerman (2008) emphasize that these paradoxes should be accepted, embraced, and transcended, not resolved. These paradoxes are fundamental challenges of working collaboratively within and outside of networks.

2.4 The Challenges of Collaborative Leadership

Leadership is critical to activating and sustaining a collaborative culture that will encourage and support working across political and organizational boundaries. The contemporary leadership literature points out the limits of the "great man," heroic, and "leader as sage" perspectives. The biggest problem with these traditional views of leadership is that they are concepts that reside exclusively in the individual. Tied in with this, the perspective is often narrowly locked into a leader-follower-shared goals triad (Drath, McCauley, Palus, Van Velsor, O'Connor, and McGuire, 2008).

Leadership in collaborative governance arrangements is contrasted to these traditional views of leadership in Table 2. Elliott and Salamon (2002) observed that collaboration and collaborative governance shift the emphasis from the control of large bureaucratic organizations and the bureaucratic way of managing public programs to facilitation and enablement skills. These enablement skills are used to bring people together, to engage partners horizontally, and to bring multiple collaborators together for a common end in a situation of interdependence. Examples of key collaboration skills include negotiation, facilitation, collaborative problem-solving, and conflict management.

Collaborations dedicated to the type of large-scale and cross-sector public policy problems such as those analyzed in this Element usually do not emerge spontaneously:

> Someone has to call the initial meeting and decide who should attend. The group needs to figure out how to organize its work, perhaps seek out new members, decide what it will do collectively, and most importantly find resources to get initial efforts going, even if the resources are something as simple as finding meeting space and getting permission to perform these new activities as part of regular job duties. Network members do not automatically embrace the idea of giving up autonomy or willingly embrace the need to work together, and often are reluctant to subsume their goals to those of the larger network. Participating in a network may carry risks and certainly imposes costs on participation. Accordingly, network governance has a distinctly emergent character, and requires a requisite amount of *collaborative leadership* on behalf of the whole network to initiate processes that inspire, nurture, support, and facilitate communication and involvement by members (e.g., individuals and organizations) in governance processes. (Imperial, Ospina, Johnston, O'Leary, Thomsen, Williams, and Johnson, 2016)

Table 2 Traditional (bureaucratic) versus collaborative leadership

Traditional	Collaborative
Vision is possessed and articulated by the leader	Helps craft collective vision
Leader frames the problem and solution for followers	Helps others frame a collective definition of the problem and appropriate solutions
Leader has to have followers to lead	Leader is simultaneously a follower
Unilateral decision-making based on hierarchy, formal position, or legal authority	Shared decisions and values
Communication within a single organization or homogeneous group with shared interests or values	Communication across diverse groups with competing interests and values
Working within boundaries (e.g., program, organization, jurisdiction)	Working across boundaries
Focus on certainty	Tolerates and embraces ambiguity and complexity
Leader directs action	Leader facilitates and coordinates shared action
More closely aligned with transactional theories of leadership	More closely aligned with charismatic or transformational theories of leadership

Imperial, Ospina, Johnston, O'Leary, Thomsen, Williams, and Johnson (2016)

As a collaborative endeavor evolves, leadership roles also evolve. Rather than one individual always leading the network, it is typical to see different organizations and different individuals stepping forward to fulfil different leadership roles at different times. "Thus, collaborative leadership is 'decentered' with the roles for leaders distributed widely across the network" (Imperial, Ospina, Johnston, O'Leary, Thomsen, Williams, and Johnson, 2016). See Figure 1. This poses another challenge for highly centralized, strong NPM countries in which leadership and individuals' performance typically is measured in a single organizational context.

Being aware of and open to collaborative approaches can be a formidable challenge for public servants who grew up in NPM regimes. In addition, as analyzed in this section, collaborative management poses paradoxes and tensions. Tied in with this, collaborative leadership is a new way of thinking and

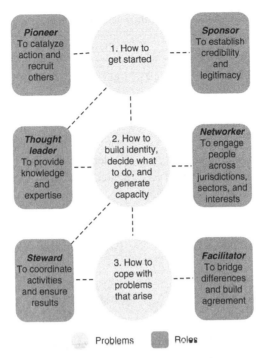

Figure 1 Collaborative leadership roles as network governance evolves

Source: Imperial, Ospina, Johnston, O'Leary, Thomsen, Williams, and Johnson (2016)

operating for many steeped in strong NPM traditions. It is easy to understand, therefore, why collaboration may be difficult for high-change NPM countries.

In the next three sections, we move from the general to the specific, examining collaboration struggles and successes in New Zealand.

3 New Zealand, the NPM Poster Child, But Maybe Not So for Collaboration

By the end of the 1990s, fragmentation of services because of NPM structural reforms was emerging as a problem in New Zealand, as was the focus on small, disaggregated units of delivery rather than outcomes (Schick, 1996; Scott, 2001). In this section, we first take a critical look at some of the ways the New Zealand government tried to tinker with laws, policies, and organizational practices to address how working across agency boundaries on crosscutting public challenges had become fraught with disincentives and barriers. Next, we examine "collaboration under the radar" by New Zealand public servants who attempted to solve pressing public policy problems by using a collaborative approach clandestinely when the NPM failed them. Finally, we examine additional impediments to collaboration in New Zealand because of NPM. The lens through which we examine these phenomena is a combination of our own on-the-ground experience with NPM reforms, as well as our own and others' scholarly research.

3.1 Tinkering with the NPM Model to Facilitate Collaboration

Beginning in the year 2000, the New Zealand government – both centrally and through individual departments – tried multiple interventions to address the NPM problems outlined in Section 2. The interventions were named Pathfinder, Mosaics, Managing for Outcomes (MFO), and Better Public Services (BPS), among others. Some of the initiatives had modest – but limited – success. For example, an early focus led agencies to share more information across government and to foster greater dialogue and discussion among public organizations, while still retaining their organizational foci (Lips, O'Neil, and Eppel, 20111. For programs dealing with the most at-risk communities with complex needs, there were attempts to have government and nongovernment service providers work together. This was especially the case in policy areas concerning housing, education, justice, and income support, as well as child and family services (Eppel et al., 2008; SSC, 2002).

Government officials trying to work across agencies found it difficult to juggle the vertical demands and accountabilities of their own organization with the need to share information and resources across agencies to close service delivery gaps (Gill et al., 2007; SSC, 2002). One example is an attempted collaboration among the Ministry of Social Development, local governments, and service providers in numerous place-based initiatives to assist at-risk teenagers to make a successful transition from school to employment. These initiatives met with mixed success because the central government set the goals and controlled the interventions, mostly ignoring local knowledge and expertise (MSD, 2013). This was the case even when there was an official mandate from both ministers and agency chief executives to work across boundaries to improve service to the public in these areas.

Another example that demonstrates the New Zealand government's failure to collaborate when needed because of NPM constraints concerns Māori, New Zealand's indigenous people. Despite the 1840 Treaty of Waitangi, which provided a constitutional foundation for New Zealand governance and guaranteed equitable outcomes for its Māori citizens, 150 years of government services had clearly not achieved this. Most statistics – such as levels of education, employment outcomes, health status, and imprisonment rates – demonstrated poor outcomes for the Māori people. In response, Māori leaders campaigned for a more holistic approach to service delivery: they wanted more design of services by Māori for Māori. In 2010, a new government in coalition with a Māori-based political party was convinced to adopt such an approach in a program called "Whānau Ora," loosely translated as "family health and well-being."

Whānau Ora did not fit easily into the siloed structures of New Zealand's NPM government departments. The new approach demanded the development of innovative ways of thinking about the purchase of services, as well as more integrated delivery agents on the ground who could package public services to meet local needs. Initially Whānau Ora had many critics. It struggled because of NPM constraints that discouraged collaboration across program and ministry boundaries to achieve the necessary flexibility over service design and public accountability. Despite challenges, Whānau Ora survived; however, it required a wholesale rethinking of how to design service delivery and accountability to better serve the needs of recipients. Its later success is chronicled in Section 4.

Pressures following the global financial crisis of 2008 triggered more tinkering with NPM when the New Zealand government instituted a program called Better Public Services (BPS). Under BPS, the government set goals and targets in ten areas for the kinds of joined-up citizen-centric results they wanted to see in response to complex problems. Examples of collaborative goals included more young people being qualified for employment and then hired for jobs, more children being vaccinated, and lower rates of reoffending. To be met, all the targets required actions from more than one agency. Across the nine years they operated, the result areas and targets had some success in engendering collaboration across agencies to meet targets.

A new political party took over in 2018 and subsequently abandoned the BPS approach. Instead, it embarked on a review of how public services generally are arranged and whether they are meeting the changing and complex needs of the people of New Zealand. One significant step was to reconfigure the annual budget around five well-being measures from creating opportunities for business to halting child poverty. In the area of child poverty, the new government took an additional step in legislating how to measure child poverty. In addition, they initiated a government-wide plan to achieve specific outcomes and funded numerous new areas to support their achievement. Time will tell whether these measures are successful in catalyzing collaboration across boundaries in New Zealand.

3.2 Collaboration under the Radar

To date, each successive initiative to adjust the basic working arrangements under NPM has had only marginal or mixed success. When there are successes, they often involve "workarounds" (going around the system) to enable accommodation under NPM. Often New Zealand frontline workers have preferred to keep their collaborative workaround efforts secret or "under the radar" because of the need to bend or break their own agency's rules to make the joined-up effort work. The thinking is often that it is easier to ask forgiveness if challenged than seek permission beforehand. In this way, they avoid risking a veto of their action or an official sanction. Their actions appear to involve a calculated risk, taken by an experienced public servant with trusted collaborators in other agencies whose help is needed, for the sake of a better outcome.

One New Zealand emergency social service frontline worker described in his own words an incident that serves as a good example of collaboration under the radar:

> When an ex-prisoner arrives from overseas on [a] Friday afternoon, without money or accommodation, and no bank account or tax number, I have two choices. Either I can … follow the rules and tell them to come back on Monday after they have obtained a tax number from an office on the other side of town (that will be closed by the time they get there), or I [can] ring a colleague at the tax office and get them to provide me a tax number so that I [can] arrange an emergency payment and temporary accommodation for the person, on the understanding that we will sort the formal paper work out on Monday. It's not following the rules, but the person gets the help they need. The alternative is [that] I close my eyes to the fact that they will need to sleep rough and probably break the law again to survive the weekend. I trust my colleague at the Tax Office, and they trust me.… [We both trust] that we will sort out the formal stuff on Monday. (Eppel et al., 2008)

If people who work in New Zealand central government agencies see a need for collaboration, they usually do not talk openly about doing it and do not label it "collaboration." Rather, they choose to operate quietly behind the scenes at or near the frontline interface with those needing government services (Eppel et al., 2008). An example of this comes from the frontline staff of social services agencies struggling to do the right thing for an extended family that had experienced several youth suicides in a short period of time.

> The family came en masse to the office of the social services and employment agency demanding financial help. The meeting was degenerating into a stand-off. While the family demanded what they thought they needed and were entitled to, the government agencies (health, social welfare, education and housing) also each had their own set of demands and conditions. For instance, housing wanted their rent paid and damage to houses to be fixed. They also wanted overcrowding of the house caused by additional visitors to cease. Police wanted a promise [that the families would] not to hold noisy mass gatherings in the street near the family house. Education wanted the parents

involved to make their children attend school. The Work and Income agency wanted the adults to seek work and operate within a budget to contain their needs to prevent applications for additional emergency grants. The meeting that day came to a halt when one of the elder grandmothers from the family called everyone out for failing to listen to the others and understand both sides. Following some offline discussion between the grandmother and one of the senior officials to try and find a way forward, the meeting was reconvened several days later using different ground rules. Each group got to put forward their perspective and slowly some common ground for compromise and a start was found. The parents with children undertook to see that their children went to school. Emergency benefits were paid to defray costs of funerals and other costs arising from the deaths and new, more appropriate, housing was made available suitable to the size of the extended families. The perspectives of the people needing the help were critical in getting the services better calibrated and sequenced in ways that met the families' needs as well as the policy objectives of the government agencies. Deals such as 'we will see that our children attend school' were struck in return for government agencies being more accommodating and working together with the families. (Gill, 2007; Eppel et al., 2008: 59–60)

One group of researchers documented a range of activities among these public servants from low-keyed simple communication ("I tell you what I am doing, and you do the same"), to cooperation and coordination when agencies sequence and mesh their actions through a deliberate, yet unstated, interconnected and interdependent process leading to collaboration. When collaboration rises up from underground in New Zealand, however, it is often cut off as not complying with standard operating procedure (O'Leary, 2014). Thus, collaboration and collaborative efforts are often hidden.

According to Eppel, Gill, Lips, and Ryan (2013: 61), among the vital ingredients for successful collaboration under the radar in New Zealand are "public entrepreneurs" with a deep public service motivation; "fellow travelers" or like-minded people with whom to work; "guardian angels" or people who can mentor, protect, advise, and advocate for the collaborators; and a client who is an active and fully engaged coproducer. O'Leary (2014) interviewed some of Eppel et al.'s guardian angels and concluded that many New Zealand public servants leave the central government or move to new agencies when their guardian angels can no longer give them the protected space they need to collaborate under the radar, or when their room to maneuver closes down because of NPM constraints.

3.3 Additional Impediments to Collaboration in New Zealand

Clearly, there are enduring challenges to collaboration under NPM. Some may be traced to the original blueprint of NPM. Others are based in the implementation of

NPM. Still others are rooted in country culture. The following highlights the most salient impediments to collaboration in New Zealand under NPM.

3.3.1 Collaboration Is Not in the NPM Vocabulary and Often Is Not Defined Today

The very notion of collaboration has been a journey of discovery for New Zealand under NPM. The NPM reforms were tightly focused on efficiency and accountability, arising as they did in a time of high national debt and low productivity (Treasury, 1987). They were strongly influenced by belief in a linear accountability relationship between purchaser and provider. The possible need for collaboration across multiple departments to address challenges that are more complex and to achieve outcomes that are more complex did not register high on the original NPM reform agenda (Boston, 2012).

It was also assumed that individual disaggregated outputs, once reaggregated, would add up to measurable outcomes (Scott, 2001; Scott, Bushnell, and Sallee, 1990). Compounding the problem is the fact that during the strongest period of NPM reform in New Zealand, if departments pointed out gaps in complex services (e.g., how could school truancy be dealt with when individual schools lacked the incentives to do so), they were chastised by Treasury and State Services Commission officials for being "captured" by those they served (Butterworth and Butterworth, 1998; Eppel and Allen, in press; Norman, 2003;). It took a decade for such gaps in service to be recognized and addressed as legitimate concerns. As problems rooted in NPM became known, the need to collaborate across boundaries to better serve the public became more obvious (Cosgrave, Bishop, and Bennie, 2003).

When New Zealand officials finally did attempt to foster collaboration officially, there were inconsistent uses of the term (O'Leary, 2014). Indeed, there were, and still are, multiple, sometimes conflicting, definitions in use in New Zealand policy guidance. As mentioned in Section 2, O'Leary also documented hundreds of instances of the State Services Commission's use of the terms "collaboration," "collaborate," "collaborative," "co-produce," and "co-production" without definition (2014: 34-40).

3.3.2 Silo Accountabilities Work against Collaboration

Chief executives and organizational accountabilities to ministers reinforce organizational silos. This, in turn, creates incentives to focus on short-term interests and those of the incumbent government to the exclusion of longer-term and more challenging outcomes (like climate change and aging infrastructure [Boston, 2016]). Experimentation with new ways of working and new services requiring codesign across agencies have been avoided when possible, because of the uncertain results, the risk of failures, and the unclear boundaries and responsibilities they created. The preference of ministers and departments has been to stick to known standard services even when they were not achieving the needed difference.

The way to succeed for many New Zealand public servants has been to devote their lives to one organization, master its subject matter (only) and then go on to lead another organization. Many career public servants have become "company men and women" who are loyal to their own organizations described by some as "hunkered down silos" (O'Leary, 2014: 26). Put another way:

> The main criticism to emerge from the [NPM] reforms is around the way agencies have developed into silos and become overly protective of their policy, information, and operations. What gets lost in the fragmentation is the collective action required to deliver the common good. (Morrison, 2014: 5)

Tied in with this, the contracts of New Zealand government chief executives up to December 13, 2013, did not formally emphasize leading across boundaries, but generally concentrated on managing and leading within one's own organization. This yielded what O'Leary (2014: 33) calls a very narrow "great man theory of leadership," with one feature being a unitary focus on one's organization and one great leader directing the charge. Again, this makes collaboration difficult.

> For the most part, agencies have been able to comply without fundamentally changing the way they operate or give up significant benefit to the greater cause. The quick wins from simple forms of collaboration are important and relevant. But the real challenge lies at the ambitious end of the spectrum where complex social, environmental and economic issues demand levels of collaboration that confront and challenge the institutional culture and arrangements of the last two to three decades. (Morrison, 2014: 3)

Indeed, the remnants of these NPM institutional reforms endure today. O'Leary analyzed managers who shied away from collaboration because of their bosses' excessive focus on accountability and performance measurement, saying that the transaction costs were too high. "It [collaboration] is a lot of work, there are no templates or examples, there is no leadership, there is no time, and there is a great fear that collaboration will not yield better outcomes," said one New Zealand public servant (O'Leary, 2014: 27).

"Collaboration will mess up my performance metrics," said another manager. When asked why he did not advocate a change in how to measure performance to his superior, the response was, "I am sure you understand the concept of knowing one's place in one's organization" (O'Leary, 2014: 27).

A high-level SSC official who said he is "well aware" of the "silo mentality" in the New Zealand bureaucracy put it this way:

> We grew up in this culture. Government workers in their 50s know nothing else. Despite discussion to the contrary, the reforms of 1980s and 1990s are still alive. Adjusting those reforms now for today's challenges and problems is a major concern. Despite dedicated individuals, agency culture can bring you down. (O'Leary, 2014: 34)

3.3.3 A Risk-Averse Culture

NPM in New Zealand has created an organization culture where it is not okay to try new things like collaboration for fear of failure. Tight accountability relationships between ministers and the chief executives of their departments, as well as chief executives and their staff, contribute to a risk-averse culture in the New Zealand public service. This culture makes it easier for an individual official to follow the rules rather than innovate for improvement and risk failure. When collaborations have been initiated through top-down mandates, they often have failed to make significant inroads on the problems because it is easy for individual agencies to "smile and nod" their agreement while defaulting to their "standard operating procedures" and organizational administrative rules rather than adopting and adapting to new ways suited to the outcomes the collaboration was seeking to achieve.

One manager put it this way, "As I read the … State Services Commission document 'Managing for Outcomes: Guidance for Departments,' I must show a return on investment for all collaborative activity. There are opportunity costs of doing things differently. I have a family. I have a mortgage. I cannot take the risk" (O'Leary, 2014: 34).

Tied in with this, fear is an inhibitor of collaboration in New Zealand; fear of the loss of power, loss of credibility, loss of control, suboptimal outcomes, loss of resources, personal loss, and loss of authority. "I have everything to lose and nothing to gain by collaborating," a program manager said. "Collaboration is a risk." Another said, "With performance indicators, I have no incentive to take risks" (O'Leary, 2014: 37). Another former CE agreed, but offered a different perspective:

> We did this to ourselves. We created an accountability system where we set targets and we said, "We will meet those targets." When we don't meet the targets, we don't want to have to explain ourselves. This is a form of arrogance. Private firms fail all the time and explain why. Public servants have become risk averse because of the stringent accountability system created years ago [under the NPM]. (O'Leary, 2014: 38)

3.3.4 Difficulty Delivering the Message

Many lament the difficulty of communicating the importance of collaboration throughout the bureaucracy. "It [the central government] is like the Catholic Church. What the people at the top think they are doing and what is actually happening is quite different. There are translation problems and transfer problems," said a high-level SSC official. The Catholic Church analogy arose again in an interview with an NGO advocate who said that the "CEs collaborate (and compete) and understand the importance of collaboration, but then as you go down the food chain less is done and less is understood" (O'Leary, 2014: 34).

In the meantime, many middle managers weary of years of government reforms are asking, "Is collaboration just another management fad? Can I dig my heels in and sit this one out?" Despite studies that point to a positive link between collaboration and performance, many New Zealand public servants don't appear to heed this message.

3.3.5 Government Financial Management Challenges

NPM has produced a government financial operating model that does not favor collaboration. In the early NPM period, this model was a process of annual departmental budget allocations, three-year forecasts, and annual reporting with unspent money at the end of a financial year returned to the government. More recently, this has been extended to a four-year cycle of annually updated budgets. The government budget consists of a series of votes under the control of a minister and administered by a government department. Each vote is made up of a collection of outputs, and the outputs are allocated to particular agencies to deliver. The very rigid and tightly managed nature of this process has consistently been identified as a barrier to across agency working (Eppel et al., 2013; Gill and Ryan, 2011; O'Leary, 2014). This is still the case today.

This process presented a major hurdle to be overcome in the funding and administrative arrangements for Whānau Ora, for example, and some modifications had to be made to enable cross-organization collaboration with Māori organizations. In this case, the service design came from the bottom up to meet the needs of the Māori community and the one-size-fits-all approach dictated by NPM was rejected.

3.3.6 Lack of Funding for Collaborative Projects

Funding for collaborative projects requires any agencies deciding to collaborate to first identify and allocate a part of their existing funding for output delivery to the collaboration. There is no direct funding for collaborative projects. This might mean that departments need to decide which of their existing services to curtail to divert funding to a collaborative endeavor. Their flexibility to do this is further constrained by predetermined outputs.

Therefore, it is often difficult for a collaborative to decide to arrange services differently because the budget and accountability arrangements for existing funding dictate what is possible. Thus, while a collaborative is trying to join up various agencies' activities to solve a cross-boundary problem, the budget rules applying to the individual agencies tend to limit what is possible. This output framing also gives the collaborative at least a perception of the agency responsible for funding wielding more power in the collaborative, which in turn sometimes silences voices that might be suggesting alternative approaches. The alternative approach might work better but often fails to be adopted because it does not fit the dominant agency's output framing.

For example, in the case of the youth employment social sector trials, the lead agency with the funding insisted on operating procedures that suited its organization only (MSD, 2013). This is often the situation where one agency has sufficient power to attempt to dominate how the collaborative works. In many instances, this causes potential and actual collaborators, needed to help produce the outcomes, to withdraw their good will and cooperation.

3.3.7 Disconnects between National and Local Levels of Government

The NPM reform legislation targeting local governments has limited the ability of local governments to collaborate, particularly in areas of social and economic policy, exacerbating preexisting tensions between national and local governments. Large areas of government social action – education, welfare, unemployment income support and assistance, and social housing – are the responsibility of central government agencies. There is little connection with local government in these areas, even though the issues keenly affect local jurisdictions. Through local and place-based networks, local governments often have incentives to solve these problems, but they are not usually included by the central government in decision-making.

In environmental matters, the regional councils (or the relevant unitary authority) are responsible for implementation of the main New Zealand environmental law, the Resource Management Act of 1992. In this case, the disconnect operated the other way around: between 1992 and 2014, there was no guidance from the central government to the regional councils about how they might implement the legislation. This resulted in each regional council designing its own process, with little collaboration across the councils or with the central government. This has proved both problematic for industries and organizations needing to work across territorial boundaries, and there has been duplication of resources and efforts. The rules that were developed were sometimes contested, requiring adjudication in the Environment Court. We elaborate further on some of the effects this had on collaboration in Section 5.

3.3.8 The Media

The nature of problems requiring collaboration across government is that they often have a public profile that draws the attention of the news media, especially in an environment that is not tolerant of experimentation and learning from doing. The sensationalist media in New Zealand is an inhibitor of collaboration, as it is perceived as constantly looking for a story of a government agency bungling or wasting public money. "If we try and fail, it will be on the first page of the newspaper," lamented a chief executive (O'Leary, 2014: 37).

In conclusion, drawing on our own participant observations and research, as well as the research of others, this section took a critical look at some of the ways the New Zealand government tried, with limited success, to tinker with laws, policies, and operational practices to address NPM problems. Next, we examined "collaboration under the radar" by New Zealand public servants as ways to work around NPM constraints. Finally, we examined additional impediments to collaboration in New Zealand, including the fact that collaboration is not a word in the NPM vocabulary, the fact that collaboration often is not defined or is defined inconsistently, a lack of knowledge about how to collaborate, silo accountabilities, the difficulty in delivering the collaboration message in an NPM bureaucratic culture, government financial management, a focus on short-term problems to the detriment of long-term challenges, a risk-averse culture, disconnects between national and local levels of government, and a sensationalist media. We conclude that NPM reforms have created incentives against, and a fear of, collaboration. In the next two sections, we explore in more detail examples of how people working across New Zealand have found their way through some of the challenges we have discussed and have been able to collaborate despite NPM.

4 Collaborating in Spite of the System

In the previous section, we noted how the NPM-type system of governance adopted in New Zealand makes collaboration hard. Nine case studies collected by Eppel et al. and the interviews conducted by O'Leary confirmed that while collaboration under this form of governance happens, it is not necessarily recognized, encouraged, or rewarded (Eppel et al., 2008; 2013; O'Leary,

2014). When collaboration does occur, it is usually because individuals or organizations recognize that they cannot, by themselves, achieve the results they want because they need the information, perspectives, and resources of others to achieve results. Getting these collaborations started and sustained is difficult because the NPM governance system is not set up to fund and manage cross-organizational efforts. Also, the skills of knowing how to collaborate and manage collaborations tend to be those of individuals rather than a competency of the public sector as a whole, which means that collaborative efforts often are inadequately led and governed. Accountability arrangements for collaborations tend to default to the traditional NPM type concerning only individual organizations and thus can undermine collaborative efforts.

Despite these issues, collaborative efforts have continued and over time have won some wider recognition that there is a place, and indeed a need, for collaboration to make progress on socially complex problems and seemingly intractable areas. In this section and the next, we have selected case studies in which collaboration successfully has risen "above the radar" in New Zealand in order to explore how these have worked in the NPM governance system. We note some adaptation of the NPM arrangements to allow for these more collaborative efforts as well as remaining abrasion points. Two of the cases in this section, Whānau Ora and the Better Public Services (BPS) Justice System result areas – briefly introduced in prior sections – were national initiatives. The third case, The Southern Initiative (TSI), is the work of one large local council, the Auckland City Council.

4.1 Whānau Ora

The Whānau Ora (family health and well-being) program reflects a philosophy of the development of holistic well-being in a multigenerational family group. The idea for Whānau Ora came from Māori, New Zealand's indigenous people, with the aspiration of changing the poor record of government social services delivery and of meeting Māori needs effectively. As a concept, Whānau Ora had a long gestational period in the world or sphere of the Māori people and their culture. In 1840, with the signing of the Treaty of Waitangi by Queen Victoria's representative and many of the Māori chiefs, Māori were promised equitable treatment and outcomes with settlers, among other guarantees. Today, most conclude that those guarantees were not honored, and egregious disparities exist in health, welfare, and education outcomes for Māori.

Whānau Ora informed the health goals of the 1999–2008 Labor government policy, He Korowai Oranga, although it lacked support in terms of Māori values and ways of working. It also did not connect to factors outside of the health portfolio – including housing, employment, and education – that are known to affect health outcomes (Smith, Moore, Cumming, and Boulton, 2019; Taskforce on Whānau-centred Initiatives (TWCI, 2010). Contrasted to He Korowai Oranga, today's Whānau Ora program aimed for a more holistic approach and was built on the principles of:

- Nga kaupapa tuku iho (the ways in which Māori values, beliefs, obligations, and responsibilities are available to guide whānau in their day-to-day lives)
- Whānau opportunity
- Best whānau outcomes
- Whānau integrity
- Coherent service delivery
- Effective resourcing, and
- Competent and innovative provision.

It was also based on the desired outcomes of whānau: self-management, achieving healthy lifestyles, participating fully in society, confidently participating in te ao Māori (the sociocultural and linguistic world of Māori), and economic security and wealth creation, in ways that are cohesive, resilient, and nurturing (Taskforce on Whānau-centred Initiatives [TWCI, 2010]). At its heart, the Whānau Ora program aims to support whānau and iwi initiatives to improve Māori outcomes.

The political opportunity for Whānau Ora to become a more widely embraced social policy approach occurred when a Māori political party joined a coalition government after the 2008 election by offering the major party support in return for advancing key Māori initiatives including Whānau Ora (Humpage, 2017; Smith et al., 2019). In the first phase of implementation (2009–10), despite the advice of the Māori-led Taskforce on Whānau-centered Initiatives that an independent trust be formed, Whānau Ora was implemented by a government department: Te Puni Kōkiri, widely referred to by its initials TPK and only rarely by its English name, the Ministry of Māori Development. The major elements of this first phase were building the capability of (predominantly Māori) providers to deliver, based on Whānau Ora principles, to their clients, and to create more integrated contracting across health and social services agencies. A Whānau Innovation, Integration and Engagement initiative (WIIE) was established to fund whānau directly in their efforts to build capability and to strengthen whānau connections.

Individual whānau themselves determined what success looked like in these projects, and worked with service providers to achieve it. Ten Regional Leadership Groups (RLGs) were formed and made responsible for leading change while representing Whānau Ora at the local level. Efforts began during this phase to train a unique workforce of Whānau Ora Navigators. The job of Navigators is to work intensively with fifteen or more marginalized whānau (families) each year who may lack the advocacy or literacy skills to navigate the complexities of government services (Boulton, 2019; Controller and Auditor General, 2015).

Despite the innovation and success of this latter element, the initial phase appears to have been limited by its focus on the health and social sectors to the exclusion of employment and education opportunities (Boulton, 2019). It was also limited by the features of the wider public sector management environment in which TPK operated, including contracting, funding, accountability, and monitoring arrangements that were insufficiently changed to meet the challenges and expectations of Whānau Ora (Controller and Auditor General, 2015; Dormer, 2014). There was no official evaluation of the first phase of the program, and the newness of the approach left it open to a continuing stream of skepticism about its success.

In response to criticisms, an important innovation was created for the second phase of Whānau Ora: Commissioning Agents (CAs). CAs are an alternative to the traditional method of funding social services in New Zealand. In the past, funding for sectors such as education, housing, health, or social welfare was managed by individual ministries or departments, reinforcing government silos. The CA idea changed this by appointing two commissioning agents (one for each main island) for Whānau Ora to direct funding as needed to achieve the Whānau Ora policy objectives by working with and through whānau and effective social service providers. A third CA for Pacific people was added later. The intent of CAs is to provide funding support to build the capability of whānau and to act as brokers in matching whānau needs with initiatives that would assist them.

Even though the CA initiative was less than the independent trust Māori had asked for, two things appear to have been achieved through this step. First, the CAs were able to develop new approaches to contracting and accountability. Second, ministers and government agencies were able to distance themselves from the risk associated with innovation and potential for failure (Boulton, 2019). The governance of Whānau Ora in this phase was moved away from TPK alone and placed in the hands of a Whānau Ora Partnership Group comprised of six representatives of the Māori Iwi Chairs Forum and six ministers of the Crown (Business, Innovation and Employment, Education, Finance, Health, and Social Development). This step was intended to enable new institutional and accountability arrangements through a partnership between Māori and the Crown.

Smith and colleagues have judged Whānau Ora a successful policy in political and programmatic terms, as well as in enduringness (Smith et al., 2019). Yet today it remains an ongoing work in progress. Fulfilling Māori expectations of the principles and outcomes for Whānau Ora has required innovation and adaptation of the core NPM model of public management, particularly as it applied to funding and accountability of individual government agencies. Māori trust in collaboration with government remains fragile and has been undermined by government failing to do as its Whānau Ora advocates suggested. Exacerbating the situation is the ongoing critical scrutiny of the media focused on finding examples of funding misuse or waste, as well as by government not providing the expected levels of funding. In one instance, for example, the central government rerouted funding to core government department programs. In another instance, the government decided against integrating the programs for rehabilitating offenders in the community, run by Māori and under the direction of Māori, as originally planned. Instead, the central government funded programs run by the Department of Corrections (DOC) that many believe have failed the Māori in the past. Overall, however, Whānau Ora is a success story in terms of modest collaborative programmatic success and improved Māori outcomes such as health, education, and employment (Smith et al., 2019).

4.2 Better Public Services: Justice Sector

In 2012, the government was facing the effects of the global financial crisis. In response, and in lieu of across-the-board funding and staffing cuts, the Prime Minister announced that the Better Public Services (BPS) program central government would set specific and measurable targets for ten areas of importance to New Zealand citizens and businesses. The government's aim was to demonstrate its expectations that the public sector must collaborate across sectors to achieve measurably better results. Achieving more with the same resources, spurring innovation, encouraging the adoption of new approaches, and accelerating the pace of state sector reforms also were articulated goals. One State Services analyst, Ross Boyd, put it this way:

> While government departments are very good at producing what ministers want of a department, they are not so good at working across portfolios. BPS was a non-structural way of getting departments to collaborate. Ministers set result targets for sectors and in order to achieve those outcomes the agencies had to collaborate. (Boyd quoted by Scott, 2018: 3:12–3:37)

Two of the ten targets were focused on the justice sector and reducing crime: specifically, result seven required a reduction in the rates of total crime, violent crime, and youth crime. Result eight required a reduction in the rate of recidivism. Using 2011 as the baseline year, public sector agencies involved in the

Justice sector (Ministry of Justice, Department of Corrections, NZ Police, Serious Fraud Office, Crown Law and Ministry of Social Development [for youth justice]) were expected to work together to achieve a set of challenging targets. These were:

- Reduce the crime rate by 15 percent by 2017;
- Reduce the violent crime rate by 20 percent by 2017;
- Reduce the youth crime rate by 5 percent by 2017; and
- Reduce the recidivism rate by 25 percent by 2017.

There were no new funds provided. Agencies were expected to do more with the same resources by collaborating. "These targets changed the goal posts for the justice sector departments because suddenly they were responsible for things they did not have direct control over" (Scott, 2018: 3:48–4:02).

A cross-sector Leadership Board consisting of the chief executives of the Justice sector agencies was formed to drive performance across the sector and to deliver on its targets. The Board also catalyzed collaboration with other social sector agencies, local governments, and NGOs to achieve the targets. The board met monthly and reported jointly to a collection of sector ministers. Chief executives were supported operationally by their deputies. As a first step, a sector action plan for target delivery was developed collaboratively by the agencies and published in July 2012.

There was some low-hanging fruit easily reached by agencies focusing initially only on their own area of influence. The progress results for March 2013, for example, showed the following: The crime rate was reduced by 1 percent, violent crime rate was reduced by 7 percent, youth crime rate was reduced by 18 percent, and the recidivism rate was reduced by 9 percent. Sector leaders told ministers they had focused on meeting the BPS targets through initiatives to prevent crime, to reduce harm, and to provide better justice services. Among the most prominent initiatives were the following:

- Police had redirected significant resources to frontline crime prevention activity. Thirty-three neighborhood-policing teams were focused on effective justice sector interventions for high-risk areas. The police mobility rollout helped focus effort where it was most needed. A shared program of work across social and justice sectors was focused on reforming alcohol regulation as a significant contributor to crime rates.
- Court services were improved by simplifying court processes, and pilot projects were established in Auckland and nearby Waitakere, dealing with alcohol and other drug offenses.

- The Department of Corrections focused on rehabilitation and reintegration services. Examples included the short gains education program that builds numeracy and literacy skills in prisoners and the work-ready programs that deliver workplace skills, financial literacy, and computer skills modules.
- Probation staff delivered alcohol and drug interventions as well as relapse prevention services and motivational interventions to offenders.
- The Police's Victim Focus initiative enabled police to focus their response on repeat victims of crime and to strengthen the level of support these victims received. Police also appointed district victims managers in each police district to better support repeat victims.
- The Ministry of Justice increased its investment in the Safe@Home program, which increases the security of domestic violence victims' homes.

Achieving the next level of results, however, required more interorganizational collaboration, presenting many challenges:

> The biggest problem in agencies working together is reconciling individual agencies' accountabilities in achieving the wider outcome. Ministers have priorities they want their agency to achieve and these need to be worked in with sector priorities." Deputy CEO, Ministry of Justice (Scott, 2018: 0:30–1:15).

An example of successful collaborating can be found in the transfer of offenders from police to the courts, to corrections, and then back again if needed. A collaborative approach increased the efficiency with which this can be done, assisted by technology and an audiovisual link (AVL) that is shared across all agencies in the partnership. Electronic bail monitoring was made more efficient and effective for the government by the Department of Corrections agreeing to manage the electronic bail program on behalf of the police. With the elimination of duplications this allowed, service effectiveness was achieved without an increase in resources.

Today, Many agencies continue to collaborate on initiatives to produce better results collectively. One example is the Collective Impact Toolkit, facilitated by the Department of Prime Minister and Cabinet to provide wider access to a set of techniques, case studies, and templates to help policy developers and frontline managers work across agencies and with their local communities. In particular, it contains detailed advice on public engagement in policy and implementation based on the IAP2 Framework (https://dpmc.govt.nz/sites/default/files/2020-10/policy-project-community-engagement-design-tool.pdf; https://dpmc.govt.nz/our-programmes/policy-project/policy-methods-toolbox). Another example is the Hutt Valley Innovation Pilot established by the Leadership Board in 2012 to identify how greater collaboration between sector agencies could better achieve the BPS targets. The result is that ten new initiatives are being implemented in the Hutt Valley, and the lessons learned from the pilot have been rolled out in the cities of Auckland, Christchurch, Dunedin, and Hamilton.

Funding transfers also have been managed across organizational boundaries. A Justice Sector Fund investment process, created from operational savings across all the agencies, has enabled the sector to reprioritize $78 million from individual agency budgets to where it is most effective in reducing crime and recidivism. The sector governance board makes decisions on how the funding will be spent and prioritized. The sector governance board has developed a formal process for directing and monitoring the cross-sector work, and senior management believe that this process, along with regular meetings and action follow-ups, has led to an increase in trust, as well as confidence across the diverse agencies in the integrity of the collaborative process. In addition, fertile ground for innovation has been created.

According to Scott (2018), the justice sector agencies achieved their results through leadership as well as systems and processes that made collaboration easier. Examples of the latter include the well-resourced secretariat staffed and paid for by all the agencies as well as quite formalized processes for approval and funding of new initiatives. Each agency needed to understand the impact of their agency's actions on the business of other agencies and programs. Senior managers talked about the need for relentless optimism, interpersonal connections, trust, compromise, and persistence in order to find common ground on which progress against the targets could be made. They report that there has not been a more powerful incentive to work together than that provided by the shared BPS targets (Scott, 2018).

4.3 The Southern Initiative

Auckland is New Zealand's largest city with a population of 1.67 million. Not surprisingly, there is a lot of diversity in this population. The Southern Initiative (TSI) is a place-based initiative established by Auckland City Council to shift outcomes in a lower socioeconomic part of Auckland that has experienced significant social and economic challenges over many years. TSI aims to build on the assets and talents of the people of South Auckland to address a range of social, economic, cultural, and environmental issues that face the community (Burkett, 2017). From its beginning, TSI developed a collaborative design and evidence-based approach to interventions in the community with the goal of bringing about transformative social and economic changes for the people living there. Its central philosophy is strengths-based and Whānau-centric programs, reflecting the belief of the community that "only the 'hood can change the 'hood'" (The Southern Initiative, 2018).

The projects facilitated by TSI focus on joining up local community groups, local employers, and education providers to obtain beneficial outcomes for all. Integral to TSI's way of working is the Auckland Co-design Lab where different groups in the community are convened by a skilled facilitator who assists the groups in actively discussing and designing their own futures. TSI considers the Lab an institutional feature for facilitating the design and testing of change and fostering innovation (The Southern Initiative, 2018).

An example of a TSI project is UPtempo, a collaborative project between TSI, the central government Ministry of Business, Innovation and Employment (MBIE), employers, and employees. It established a prototype to help transition Māori and Pacific workers in low-skilled, low-paid jobs into jobs that are higher-skilled, higher-paid, and in more-sustainable "sunrise" industries. There was a particular focus on people with jobs at-risk of automation in "sunset" industries (The Southern Initiative, 2019). In contrast to the typical governance approach under NPM where ministers and government decide what is needed and then design and fund it, in TSI needs are identified in the community, and community-based capability is brought together to design solutions in the design Lab. It is an approach that builds on the strengths and capabilities of the local community and enables those assets to be marshalled in new and innovative ways to build better social and economic outcomes for the city and the communities and families involved.

4.4 Observations about the Compatibility of NPM and Collaboration from These Cases

It takes many committed participants to collaborate successfully, and motivations to collaborate vary. Individuals and organizations come together to collaborate for a wide array of reasons, including economic, social, organizational, or political, to address cross-sector failure (Bryson et al., 2006), to leverage resources and knowledge (Graddy and Chen, 2009) for more efficient delivery of services (Agranoff and McGuire, 2003b; Bardach, 1998), to seek visibility or legitimacy, and to build collaborative relationships (O'Leary and Vij, 2012). Each of the three cases analyzed in this section exhibit many of these motivations, yet most importantly, the primary driver was to solve important societal problems that could not be solved by a single organization. Innovation and change necessitated finding ways around the strict mandates of individual organizations and formal processes of NPM as conceived and implemented in New Zealand, as well as bringing in resources and insights from the local community and government.

In each case, the institutional structures of NPM were modified to enable them to be fitted to a particular problem rather than employ the opposite typical NPM approach where the problems and services are broken up to suit arbitrary institutional boundaries. Under the NPM enhancement of the separation of policy from operations, ministers are responsible for making decisions about the problems to be addressed. As challenges become more complex, individual agencies find that they lack the information, knowledge, and resources to diagnose a problem adequately and determine solutions that will work effectively in a variety of circumstances. In all the cases profiled in this section, the two most important lessons learned involve those most affected in the design of interventions and collaborating across government and nongovernment boundaries to get traction on hard issues and solve problems in innovative ways.

In Whānau Ora, this meant involving Māori families in the design of the services they needed. This does not mean that elected decision makers in government should entirely take their hands off the tiller, however, as they have a role in motivating and even mandating the desired results (as was the case in the government's BPS targets). It means, in part, leaving room for the expert sailor (businesses, service providers, and community groups) to make use of their knowledge of the sea and the boat in order to get to the desired destination (Room, 2016). Hence, the governance board in the justice sector, drawing on its collective knowledge of the pipeline of offending and offenders, was collectively able to adjust its individual services in ways that improved the overall result without additional expenditures. TSI is formulating responses to problems current and future by codesigning interventions that will make for a more resilient community.

Each of the programs needed to develop a new institution to enable multiorganizational codesign and decision-making around its area of focus: Whānau Ora had its Partnership Group, the Justice sector had its Governance Board, and TSI had its Design Lab. In these new institutions, the organizational roles and responsibilities are not tightly constrained from the outset but rather are negotiated to bring resources and knowledge together in flexible and novel ways to address a common problem. The Whānau Ora Navigators did this with whānau and service providers and agreed with the Partnership Group how they would be held accountable. The governance board serves the Justice sector agencies in this way, and the Design Lab facilitates this with multiple community actors for TSI.

Fundamental to NPM are the institutional disciplines it created around government financial management and accountability. Each of the three cases has developed new ways of circumventing constrained funding of specific, quantifiable services typically offered by silo institutions. Under NPM we see funding for education funneled through the Ministry of Education and then on to formal existing institutions such as schools, or health funding through the Health Ministry and then on to Health Boards, for example. Fixing a problem with health and education dimensions (or others) in these arrangements must first identify the separate health and education components and then bid for resources within that portfolio. This makes for a cumbersome and inflexible response.

Both TSI and the Justice sector governance board found their own way of creating funding that could be repurposed to fit needs rather than the other way around (where needs are predetermined and services prespecified). Whānua Ora, in particular, has taken a bold step toward changing the standard NPM funding arrangement by creating CAs working outside the traditional constraints of highly specified outputs and silo accountabilities of government departments created by NPM. By empowering CAs to negotiate programmatic changes and funding, the collaborative enabled accountability to be determined by the service recipients. This is an innovation that many hope will result in better outcomes for Māori. Progress to date is promising. The CA Model has been watched closely and is seen as a possible model for wider use in delivering other services in other complex, high-need policy areas (New Zealand Productivity Commission, 2015).

In the next section we extend our analysis of retrofitting collaboration into the NPM through consideration of two additional collaborative innovations in New Zealand: The Land and Water Forum and the Canterbury Water Management Strategy. They are cases where there was a more explicit intention to take a collaborative approach, based on the work of the Nobel Prize winner Elinor Ostrom on the governance of common-pool resources such as freshwater. The way collaboration was designed and implemented in these two new cases offers further important lessons.

5 Freshwater Governance and Collaboration: A Better Way?

Freshwater governance under NPM in New Zealand is an interesting domain of the emergence of more-collaborative approaches for environmental policy and management. We provide two illustrative examples: the Land and Water Forum (LAWF), from the national policy governance arena, and the development and implementation of the Canterbury Water Management Strategy (CWMS), as a regional water governance collaborative. In both cases, policy and implementation progress under traditional NPM arrangements had stalled and the sector was aware of collaboration being used in other countries based on the work of Elinor Ostrom on the management of common-pool resources (Ostrom, 1990).

The LAWF involves collaboration among elite policy stakeholders to broker a way forward in a stalled national policy arena. The CWMS used collaboration first, to obtain regional consensus about the valuing of freshwater resources (which had been stymieing decision-making for at least a decade) and second, to develop detailed plans for the management of ten catchments. While both examples are areas of ongoing development, we assess what collaborative approaches have contributed to governance and note the weaknesses that have been exposed.

5.1 The Land and Water Forum

In 2009, attempts to develop a national policy for freshwater use had been stalled for over a decade (Logan, 2013. Arrangements for freshwater governance in New Zealand had evolved over decades since European settlement and the Treaty with the indigenous Māori tribes in 1840. Dingfelder, in her study of the Land and Water Forum, noted that "freshwater is a key component of New Zealand's economy for urban water supplies, energy generation, agricultural production, viticulture, horticulture, and tourism . . . [and is] also critical to New Zealand's identity and unique ecosystems" (Dingfelder, 2017: 69).

The NPM reforms brought a wide range of environmental legislation into a single law – the Resource Management Act 1991 (RMA) – and created an impact-based framework under which the natural environment should be protected. It enabled water use decisions to be made by a regulatory authority in each region – a territorial or regional council elected by the residents. The New Zealand national government provided no further guidance on how regional authorities were to conduct their decision-making processes, even though there was provision in the Act for national guidelines and policy statements.

From 1991 to 2011, without guidelines for water quality, there was also no consistency in the decision-making processes of the regional councils. The result was that water regulation throughout the country was patchy, and degradation of water quality in some regions was noticeable. Regulation of water up until this time was largely about protecting introduced fish stock such as salmon and trout from the water degradation caused by development and the alteration of natural waterways through farming, industry, extraction, and damming (Knight, 2019). Most regional councils found their ability to make decisions limited by frequent and time-consuming legal challenges in the Environment Court, either by those who wanted more relaxed approaches to water use to enable agricultural and industry development, or by those who wanted the water resources to stay unchanged for cultural, aesthetic, or recreational purposes. Knight (2019) argues that decisions of the Environmental Court during this period tended to favor farmers and development. However, the absence of guidelines gave decision makers little help regarding the public's preferences, valuing of water's multiple uses, or the extent of public license for change.

The 2001–11 period coincided with economic policies that favored regional development and rapid expansion of primary industries, particularly the dairy industry. By then, regional councils had established controls over point source pollution of water, but non–point source freshwater contamination from agricultural production and other sources presented growing challenges. With the help of irrigation schemes, often subsidized by government, land formerly used for sheep farming, forestry, and other uses was converted to dairy farms. In some areas, there was as much as a 500 percent increase in the number of dairy cows. A voluntary accord between dairy farmers and government agencies to stem the environmental effects of runoff of dairy farm contaminants into streams and rivers proved inadequate for stemming a growing water pollution problem (Tyson, 2005, 2014). Many wanted a more nationally consistent approach to regulation than the one that the regional councils, empowered by the RMA, were delivering.

Deteriorating water quality, mainly as a result of agricultural intensification and urban growth, worried many New Zealanders and environmental watchdogs (Parliamentary Commissioner for the Environment, 2015). Unfortunately, by 2008, conflict between the pro-environment groups wanting tighter environmental protection and pro-development groups wanting more access to water had stalled the policy-making processes to establish national guidelines for land and water protection and use (Logan, 2013).

New Zealand environmentalist Guy Salmon pointed to the impressive achievements of Nordic counties in making major changes to create more sustainability in infrastructure and resource use using collaborative approaches. Salmon, whom some might call a policy entrepreneur (Kingdon, 2010 Lewis 1980), introduced this model at an environment conference attended by key players representing differing positions on environmental policy (Salmon, 2008). Follow-up discussions created an opening for the application of a collaborative approach as a way of moving the stalled policy work forward. Key players from seemingly different positions, such as the large, international dairy company Fonterra and the Environmental Defense Society, backed the approach. Around the same time, the relevant government ministers, in the face of stalled policy progress, also were convinced that a different and collaborative approach to policy development could work. The idea of the Land and Water Forum (LAWF) was born: a network of interested parties collaborating actively and directly with each other to advance a workable policy to the benefit of all. The alternative was thought to be continuing conflict and stalemate, with damaging consequences for the environment and economy (Bisley, 2010; Dingfelder, 2017; Eppel, 2013; Howard-Williams, Bisley, and Taylor, 2013).

> LAWF ... was an ambitious public planning experiment to attempt a "collaborative" approach ... its genesis was the growing realization by competing interests in natural water conservation and use that this resource was in fact finite and that cumulative use by one sector was having unacceptable consequences for the aspirations of other sectors ... LAWF brought together sectors with the hope that each might gain a better appreciation of each other's interests and aspirations, and in doing so identify a way forward based on compromise. (Edwards, 2013: 2)

The ministers responsible for primary industry development and the environment provided resources for the facilitation of the collaborative processes of LAWF and the support of their departments. They undertook to listen, to consider LAWF's advice, and in the meantime, not to encourage attempts to bypass LAWF. The number of parties involved in LAWF grew to over sixty organizations with a stake in some aspects of water policy, including five iwi-Māori tribal-level organizations with significant water catchments in their tribal areas. LAWF became a collaborative policy forum for producing diverse stakeholder advice to government. The government's usual policy actors such as the Ministry for the Environment, the Ministry for Primary Industries, and the Parliamentary Commissioner for the Environment took back seats with advisory roles, played also by the National Institute for Water and Atmospheric Research (NIWA) as well as other research institutes.

In the first year, resources went into establishing constructive relationships among the LAWF members and learning how to collaborate. Within three years LAWF had produced four substantial consensus-based reports (Bisley, 2013; Dingfelder, 2017). The first two reports set out a broad new approach to the management of freshwater (Land and Water Forum, 2010, 2012a). LAWF drew on Ostrom's research on the management of common-pool resources (Ostrom, 1990), as well as examples where this approach was being applied, such as Canterbury in New Zealand. All the members of LAWF supported these first reports, and they were well received by ministers and the public.

> According to [Alastair] Bisley [the independent chair of LAWF who reported directly to ministers], the Forum process was organic. People came because they wanted to come and new people joined the process during 2009, and 2010. The Forum worked on a consensus rule. "Everyone had to agree enough not to say they disagreed." Members of the Forum were forced to reach beyond a simple yes/no. According to Bisley, whatever the Forum came out with had to have benefits for all of its members not just some. Bisley says that while this consensus rule might appear to give everyone a veto power,

actually it puts enormous pressure on everyone to find a way through. If you cannot reach consensus, says Bisley, then you have to continue to make progress by setting out the options clearly. While the Forum did reach consensus on the report as a whole, there are a few areas in the report where options are laid out for more work to be done, because a consensus was not reached. "It's also better to have more than two options, to avoid polarity," says Bisley. (Eppel, 2013: 8)

The New Zealand government adopted LAWF's broad framework in its new freshwater policy and endorsed a collaborative approach to water management in the regions (Ministry for the Environment, 2013). LAWF then needed to tackle more-contentious policy details such as the setting of environmental limits on how much the quality of freshwater resources could be altered and recognition of indigenous Māori rights granted under the 1840 Treaty of Waitangi, which promised Māori continuing governance rights over their lands, waterways, and fisheries. Over the 170 years since the signing of the Treaty, fresh water had been treated as a limitless resource, and Māori rights to freshwater had largely been ignored in the buying and selling of land and the granting of "consents" to use water. Resource consents allow people or organizations to do something that affects the natural environment. Under the RMA, one must apply for a resource consent if one wishes to do something that is not permitted by district or regional plans. Now Māori tribes wanted to be more active in protecting their water.

It had become more obvious, under accelerated development, that water is not a limitless resource. The real costs of use, as well as the maintenance of water quality, were not being recognized or fairly shared. Despite the range of views held on these difficult public policy problems among the LAWF members, the Forum managed to identify areas of agreement across all members, and on other issues to clearly articulate the policy choices and their implications (Land and Water Forum, 2012b, 2015).

LAWF continued to provide advice on water policy issues from their multi-stakeholder perspective until 2018. However, as government became more active in articulating new policy for freshwater, the cohesion of LAWF began to falter. There were areas where government was viewed by some LAWF members as cherry-picking LAWF's recommendations when the debates within LAWF had viewed them as a finely balanced set of compromises.

A central element of the process that under-pinned participation and enabled the Forum to ... finally agree on three substantive reports with 156 recommendations, was the expectation that the Government would honor the recommendations on the basis that as all the competing interests had become the architects of these recommendations the Government would have no justifiable mandate to take a substantively different path or pick winners. (Edwards, 2013: 2)

A new Minister for the Environment in 2013 facilitated a gradual distancing of ministers from LAWF and a reassertion of the predominance of ministerial decision-making on policy, as well as the preeminence of the Ministry for the Environment as the chief policy adviser. Government further undermined the stakeholder trust generated through LAWF by generating new policy proposals that had not previously been on the table and seen as substantive changes to the principles and purposes of the RMA. A change in the governing party after an election in 2017 led to even less willingness by government to listen solely to LAWF. An open but also less collaborative approach was taken as government began engaging with sectors separately to arrive at a preferred government policy position. Today, as stakeholders regroup in their traditional policy spaces post LAWF, it is uncertain whether policy progress will continue to be made or whether the processes will again become stalled as stakeholders stake, and shore up, their corners of the debate.

From 2011 to 2018, the LAWF served a much needed purpose in helping to unseize entrenched policy positions and promote mutual learnings across stakeholders. The role of the independent LAWF Chair was to facilitate and hold open the space in which collaboration on the development of new broadly accepted policy positions was possible. When the valuing of LAWF's recommendations by ministers was perceived by stakeholders to decline, then so too did the commitment to collaborate by its members. In the end, LAWF and collaboration were undermined by a return to standard NPM governance practices in which the elected Minister of Environment – and not the collective – formulates final policy decisions.

5.2 Canterbury Freshwater Management

The Canterbury Regional Council, or Environment Canterbury, usually abbreviated "ECan," is the Canterbury region's environmental regulatory authority. Canterbury, on the South Island, makes up 19 percent of New Zealand's land area: it contains the city of Christchurch, numerous small to medium-sized rural towns, and ten large river systems. Other than the city, much of the economic activity of Canterbury is farming on the plains that lie between the Southern Alps in the west and the sea in the east. Braided rivers running across the plains tend to be seasonal in their flow depending on the spring snow melt. Aquifers also fed by snow melt lie beneath the plains. Using or storing water from these sources for farming, irrigation, or other uses has increased, placing demands on ECan.

Coming into being in 1991 as part of New Zealand's NPM reforms, ECan struggled to get approval for a regional land and water plan that would provide the parameters under which it would give effect to the RMA and approve "consents" to use freshwater (Kirk, 2015). Economic and regional development policies favored increasing the scale and intensity of farming through new irrigation schemes. Yet to do this, greater certainty over year-round water was needed, creating pressure for new water consents to store water and to divert water from the rivers for irrigation to the detriment of water flow and fish spawning grounds. Opposing this were people who valued the rivers just as they were – with enough water in them to be good for fishing, water sports, and other recreational activities, and preserving their original cultural and environmental aesthetics.

These different values were reflected among the elected councillors. Every time ECan tried to have a plan approved, it was challenged and stalled. The result was that for nearly twenty years ECan defaulted to making its consent decisions on a first-come-first-served basis and without consideration of the impacts on other types of users or the overall environmental effects on the region.

Around the year 2000, a newly arrived ECan CEO initiated a process of working with the diverse freshwater stakeholders across Canterbury in an effort to achieve a more strategic and consensus-based decision-making process for managing freshwater. He too was inspired by Ostrom's 1990 work on managing common-pool resources. Experts and stakeholders shared what was known, new studies were commissioned, and ultimately, after nearly a decade of research and discussion, there was emerging support for a draft plan. Participants in the process included Māori, farmers, and recreation interests such as swimmers, fishers, and water sports enthusiasts. The idea of different people valuing freshwater differently became central to the planning process that recognized aesthetic, cultural, and recreational values as well as the economic, farming, and development uses of water. The ten mayors of the district councils that make up Canterbury, keen to have a clearer decision-making process with a view to the longer-term economic development of the region, became the champions of this plan that became known as the Canterbury Water Management Strategy (CWMS) (Salmon, 2012).

The mayors expected ECan to implement the plan, and when they feared that ECan might yet again prove unable to approve the plan, they appealed to the Minister of the Environment to dismiss the ECan-elected body and replace it. Central government took this step, appointed commissioners to take on the legislated powers of ECan, and asked them to expedite the approval of a plan. This occurred, and ECan set about implementing the CWMS in 2010.

Since 2010, ECan has approved a Regional Land and Water Plan and put in place a collaborative process in each of its ten districts to develop the details of district subsections of the plan for each catchment area, using the CWMS as its touchstone. ECan has appointed a diverse group of local people divided into Zone Committees for each catchment area to advise it on the specific valuing of bodies of water in their catchment area and the particular rules to be applied when decisions about water use are made for that catchment.

There were some tricky issues for ECan to navigate when adopting the Zone Committee reports. On the one hand, ECan commissioners have a statutory responsibility to consider the recommendations and decide whether to adopt them or not. On the other hand, the expectation of the Zone Committees and those who had participated in collaborative deliberations was that their recommendations would be accepted as a carefully considered package consisting of compromises and trade-offs based on the judgment of people closest to where the rules would take effect. The fear of the Zone Committees was that organizations and individuals with deep pockets would relitigate issues during the final hearing process leading to adoption. For the most part, this appears not to have happened. Zone Committee recommendations have by and large been adopted by ECAN as a chapter of the Canterbury Land and Water Plan that forms ECan's decision-making guide. ECan has begun reporting regularly against the targets that were set collaboratively in the CWMS (Eppel, 2015; Environment Canterbury, 2017).

When ECan embarked on its collaborative water study in 2002 with the participation of iwi, the district councils in their area, and a wide range of freshwater stakeholders, the process did much to build an informed understanding of water management issues facing ECan by a wider number of stakeholder interests (Salmon, 2012). That study turned into the well-supported CWMS and a new process of collaborative development of rules for the management of particular catchments, drawing on the values and expertise of local stakeholders as well as scientific expertise. It was implemented by ECan, and progress began to be made in applying the plan. However, the challenges were great since the legacy left by past ad hoc decisions largely favored development and overcommitment of water resources. In the words of one ECan commissioner, the state of the water in Canterbury was likely to get worse before it got better, but he believed the commitment of stakeholders gained through the collaborative Zone Committee processes would in the end assist community education and progress toward cleaner freshwater (Eppel, 2015).

Since the implementation of the CWMS began in 2010, ECan has also had to adapt to new environmental limits set in new guidelines issued by the central government. In general, these set environmental bottom lines beyond which region councils must not allow water quality to fall. This has necessitated more monitoring by regional councils. The maintenance of a national overview of water quality has been assisted by the creation of the national Environmental Reporting Act 2015. In the period 2010–13, the collaborative processes overseen by ECan were reinforced and assisted by the regulatory changes made at the national level and in part formed a working model case for the national policy.

With a change of government in 2017 came a renewed national focus on reviewing the RMA, which has reignited tensions between the pro-development groups and the pro-environment conservation groups. As mentioned in the LAWF case study, the national policy-making environment has become less collaborative after 2017. Hotly contested issues include freshwater quality and whether regional councils are working fast enough and doing enough to stem water degradation through actions like planting stream edges, fencing waterways, encouraging farming changes through environmental management plans for individual farms, and punishing breaches. The national government is considering further tightening regulatory requirements, and water users are fighting back over the perceived costs to their industry of meeting tighter requirements. This does not bode well for future collaboration at the regional level and threatens the constructive dynamic that had evolved between local collaboration and traditional NPM decision-making at regional and national levels.

An ever-present threat to collaboration is any breach of the understandings reached among the various collaborators about what will happen next. The informal and unlegislated arrangements under which collaboration has taken place in Canterbury also make it vulnerable, because there is always a risk that they might be overturned through decisions made at the national level by ministers and their departments. An additional threat has been the return of ECan to a fully elected council, which also brought with it a potential for a downward shift in ECan's commitment to collaborative processes.

5.3 Conclusion

Clearly, collaborative approaches to solving freshwater challenges in New Zealand have yielded many benefits in the form of movement on stalled policy and decision-making areas as well as widely accepted stakeholder endorsement of the broad general direction of policy. Those representing competing perspectives have been brought to the table to talk about their common interests concerning the future for water quality and use. Creative ideas for water conservation and protection have surfaced, and many are now endorsed in nationally mandated policy. Mutual education regarding different and competing perspectives on water use has occurred to the benefit of policy- and decision-making regarding water use.

The Land and Water Forum and the emergence of the Canterbury Water Management Strategy also illustrate the paradox of collaboration introduced in Section 2. They were both initiated by activists who observed the inability of national government to make progress on water policy and, in part, concluded that "the central government cannot collaborate given the [NPM] structure of New Zealand government" (O'Leary, 2014: 33). Accordingly, the ten Canterbury district mayors became the champions of the collaboratively developed CWMS, bypassing the national policy agencies. The LAWF Chair and forum members relegated representatives of the central government to the sidelines as observers during LAWF's facilitated deliberations, rather than having them in the middle of the room as full participants. Defining collaboration as "addressing complex and intractable issues by bringing together the principal stakeholders to seek agreement on a way forward," an organizer of the LAWF listed nine reasons why he thought the central government could not collaborate (O'Leary, 2014: 33). We think of these as the water in which efforts to collaborate in New Zealand swim, making progress difficult but not impossible:

- New Zealand bureaucrats are "good at implementing orders." Results are demanded too quickly, which negatively affects innovation;
- There are too many political risks to collaborating;
- Ministers order specific solutions that lack sufficient knowledge of the problem or how the solution will work;
- Public servants are beholden to ministers who are beholden to the Cabinet;
- There is a perceived lack of transparency;
- Bureaucrats protect their turf;
- Each ministry or organization would have to sign off on collaborative decisions, making changes difficult;
- There is an unevenness in terms of competence and know-how. Many public servants cannot see an advantage to collaborating; and
- There is a dearth of data, making it virtually impossible to determine the long-term costs or effects of changes on public management.

Paradoxically, when these reasons were repeated to a high-ranking central government environmental official, his response was one of shock and an adamant statement that they had indeed been collaborating with the LAWF:

> I am shocked at that statement [that the central government is incapable of collaborating]. What do they think we have been doing the last few years in the Land and Water Forum? They have received a million dollars a year from central government, a secretariat, and other resources. Representatives from several central government organizations participated. The Land and Water Forum would not have happened without the support of the central government. If that isn't collaboration, what is it? … If they [environmental advocates] think they can participate in co-production, they are naïve. Co-production would be very difficult given the New Zealand dual political process. (O'Leary, 2014: 33)

When asked what he meant by co-production, the central government official offered this definition and another strong opinion:

> [Co-production means] [d]esigning programs and expecting us to rubber stamp them. Ministers do not like to be locked in. Their degrees of freedom decrease when they are locked in. The government cannot be held hostage. (O'Leary, 2014: 34)

These colliding statements foreshadowed the current situation where the central government chooses the recommendations and ideas from LAWF it wishes to implement and ignores the rest. The same might be said for Environment Canterbury, with the additional paradox that environmental policy decisions made by ECan might be fragile and could easily be overtaken by the central government.

Both these collaborative water governance and management cases existed without a clear legislative mandate, which made default back to NPM institutions, structures, and processes always a possibility. Collaboration enabled progress that the NPM institutions and processes had failed to make. In this sense, collaborative discussion and dialogue in New Zealand, fueled by noncentral government actors, can be seen as a legitimate and effective way to bring diverse stakeholders together to generate creative ideas for solving society's most pressing public policy problems. On the other hand, the durability of decisions made solely through this type of collaboration, and without the approval of the strong NPM central government, is questionable since it has been shown how easily these efforts can be overturned. The final paradox then becomes that the central government NPM governance processes are often needed to make collaborative decisions stick. However, the history of the New Zealand NPM is that the central government, generally, is not set up to collaborate. While it might bank the gains made through collaboration, it does little to value collaborative capital for the longer term often spending it for short term political gain. This is the central dilemma and weakness of collaboration in New Zealand today.

6 What Is Needed to Retrofit Collaboration into Strong NPM Governments?

In this section, we summarize the lessons learned from our research seeking to encourage and inject more collaboration into strong NPM governments. These findings, and the work that supports them, lead us to identify several suggestions for enabling and supporting collaboration in strong NPM governments.

In Section 1, we emphasized that hundreds of jurisdictions around the world have adopted NPM ideas in order to reform government institutions. While the influence of NPM ideas remains strong today, there is no singular model of NPM. Rather, it is a spectrum of ideas with efficiency, managerial discretion on means, and accountability of public servants at its core. NPM implementation ranges from countries and jurisdictions embracing strong reform to others selectively implementing relatively small reforms.

New Zealand is a high-change NPM country, meaning it is considered one of the strongest creators, proponents, developers, and implementers of NPM in the world (Pollitt & Bouckaert, 2017). While many of the reform goals were successfully met in New Zealand, some were ignored or failed. Shortcomings include developing new ways of handling complex and controversial policy issues and enhancing horizontal coordination across governmental organizations through joined-up governance, collaborative governance, and co-management. Collaboration with nongovernmental organizations, private organizations, and the public remains underused. This makes New Zealand an ideal setting to examine the challenges of retrofitting collaborative ideas, approaches, and processes into countries imbued with NPM ideologies, and to generate lessons learned.

In Section 2 we asserted, based on theory as well as practice, that collaboration across boundaries – either in or outside of networks – can be a viable public management tool for problems that cannot be solved or easily solved by single organizations. We also emphasized that collaboration can include the public. The major theoretical reasons to collaborate include resource dependency, common purpose, shared beliefs, political interests, and catalytic actors. The major practical reasons to collaborate include the fact that most public policy challenges, particularly the gnarlier ones, extend beyond traditional agency boundaries; the need to increase public involvement; and the need to increase the effectiveness and success of policies and service delivery. Some of the biggest challenges of collaboration include differing aims and expectations of partners, differing views about strategies and tactics, power imbalances, competing loyalties to home organizations versus the collaborative, and bureaucratic constraints.

All of these reasons for, and challenges to, collaboration can be found in New Zealand. By the end of the 1990s, the limitations of New Zealand's NPM-type reforms were widely recognized, particularly how the funding and accountabilities of organizational silos and fragmentation of services, created and reinforced by the reforms, hindered collaboration. In response, the New Zealand government tried tinkering with how its NPM laws, policies, and interorganizational interactions worked to catalyze joined-up government and cross-agency solutions to pressing public problems, with limited success. Challenges arose in part due to lack of understanding and interest in collaborative management and collaborative leadership approaches.

In Section 3, we presented our finding that collaboration under NPM in New Zealand tends to be an exception rather than the rule. Collaboration often begins "under the radar" and without official endorsement largely because those on the front line see a need. Collaboration, however, was not a word in the original national NPM vocabulary. When collaboration is mentioned, it often is not defined, or has multiple definitions.

From 2000 onwards, in response to widespread realization of the NPM reform's limitations, the New Zealand government began tinkering with NPM institutions and processes to catalyze joined-up government and cross-agency solutions to pressing public problems, with limited success. The institutional culture and practices of NPM, particularly those around organizational accountability and resource management, remained too strong and brought many attempts at collaboration to an end.

In Section 4 we highlighted some administrative practice reforms New Zealand has made since 2010. The Better Public Services (BPS) program is an example that used government-set targets that needed the input of more than one agency for their achievement. The goal was to encourage public servants to think and operate across the whole government system and beyond to effectively address complex issues that have been holding New Zealand back, and to create opportunities through collaborative endeavors (Morrison, 2014: 3). Especially significant were two changes to the State Sector, Public Finance and Crown Entities Acts passed by Parliament in 2013 that were intended to make it easier for collaboration among state sector agencies to occur. Also significant were innovations such as the designation of clusters of agencies to work on the BPS five results areas collectively; functional leads for areas that affect all of government such as digital government and procurement; "heads of profession" to lead in legal, communications, policy, finance, and human resources with mandates to steer practice and performance improvements across agencies; shared services; and sector group crosscutting initiatives. Yet despite all these innovations, Morrison concluded:

While these are all good in themselves and achieving worthwhile results, there is little evidence that they are transforming the way agencies think about work and operate as a matter of course. For the most part, agencies have been able to comply without fundamentally changing the way they operate or give up significant benefits to the greater cause. The quick wins from simple forms of collaboration are important and relevant. But the real challenge lies at the ambitious end of the spectrum where complex social, environmental and economic issues demand levels of collaboration that confront and challenge the institutional culture and arrangements of the last two to three decades. (Morrison, 2014: 3)

As analyzed in Section 5, a deliberate adoption by government ministers and agencies of collaborative approaches for two water governance cases faltered when they encountered a reassertion of NPM thinking and decision-making practices, despite their success in unfreezing stalled policy and implementation.

Our conclusion from the research presented in these sections is that collaboration and NPM governance processes are uncomfortable bedmates. The NPM government budgeting model for funding public services through departments, contracting out, accountability, and monitoring favors service fragmentation. Accommodation of collaboration will require significant modification of the standard New Zealand NPM operational model as well as delivery and accountability arrangements.

A surprising find is that when the accommodation required is achieved though ad hoc arrangements, collaborations and what could be and has been achieved through them remain vulnerable to changing personnel and organizational priorities. Alternative institutions for funding, design, delivery, monitoring, and accountability are needed. Failure to create structural accommodation within the standard NPM administrative processes makes collaborations reliant on the continuing goodwill of voluntary parties. Further, the trust built up through successful collaboration can be undermined by the imposition of nonnegotiable NPM requirements. The success of these collaborations depends on continuing political support, and because of the extent to which they build work-around processes that are neither standardized, codified, nor supported in law, they remain vulnerable to the winds of political change.

In each case overviewed in Section 4 (Whānau Ora, BPS Justice System and the Southern Initiative), the institutional structures of NPM were modified to enable them to be molded to a particular problem, rather than employing the opposite typical NPM approach where the problems and services are broken up to suit arbitrary institutional boundaries. Each of the cases profiled in Section 4 illustrates two core principles introduced in Section 2. The first is that those most affected by the intervention need to collaborate in the design of the program. The second is that the collaboration often must stretch across both government and nongovernment boundaries to get traction on hard issues and solve problems in innovative ways. In each case a surprising find is that this was achieved by creating a distancing from central government and it processes. For Whānau Ora it was the use of commissioning agents. For BPS it was the setting, monitoring, and public reporting of goals and targets to be achieved by a group of agencies. For the Southern Initiative it was the use of the Design Lab to flesh out the problems to be addressed and to develop shared solutions with all the stakeholders involved.

The LAWF case further illustrates core collaboration principles introduced in Section 2 and especially emphasizes that governance and management of limited common-pool resources, such as water, can benefit from a collaborative approach in both policy development and the implementation of codeveloped regulations or requirements. Collaborative processes build shared knowledge and understanding of socially complex issues from multiple perspectives and therefore illuminate policies and designs not previously considered to create a shared desired outcome. Despite the slowness typical of collaborative planning and design during the initial phases, the process – when done right – typically yields shared understanding of issues, interests, and the benefits of alternative solutions, thereby creating some of the hallmarks of smooth implementation and sustainability.

6.1 Need for a Mandate

The water governance examples in Section 5 highlight that a mandate for a collaborative endeavor improves its odds of success in strong NPM countries. This can be achieved in different ways. The collective will can be generated through education and dialogue. This is what happened in the early stages of LAWF, CWMS, and the Canterbury Zone committees. Additionally, elected officials (ministers in the case of the LAWF, and the district mayors and ECan in the case of the CWMS) can provide legitimacy that endures as long as their political support continues.

When collaborative processes in a strong NPM system remain voluntary and unlegislated (as they typically have been in New Zealand), they are vulnerable to a withdrawal of their mandate or an undermining of their collaboratively achieved results by those with formal legislated powers. There are always abrasion points, often fueled by the collaboration paradoxes presented in Section 2, that need to be addressed to move collaborative solutions forward. In both water examples in Section 5, even though the decision to collaborate was a deliberate choice and officially supported, it existed without a clear legislative mandate, which made default back to NPM institutions, structures, and processes always a possibility.

In one sense, collaborative discussion and dialogue in New Zealand, fueled by non–central government actors, can be seen as a legitimate and effective way to bring diverse stakeholders together to generate creative ideas for solving society's most pressing public policy problems. The durability of decisions made solely through this type of collaboration, and without the approval of the central government, however, is questionable in strong NPM governments.

Another important lesson learned for strong NPM governments, then, is the paradox that the central government NPM governance processes are often needed to make collaborative decisions stick. However, the history of strong NPM-type institutions and administrative processes such as those in New Zealand is that the central government, generally, is not set up to collaborate and can be a fickle collaboration partner. This has been the central dilemma and weakness of collaboration in New Zealand, and will be in other strong NPM countries, we hypothesize.

6.2 Need for New Ways of Leading, Focusing on Constraints

In Section 2 we highlighted the essence of collaborative leadership where the emphasis is shifted from the control of large bureaucratic organizations and the bureaucratic way of managing public programs to facilitation and enablement skills. These enablement skills are used to bring people together, to engage partners horizontally across boundaries, and to bring multiple collaborators together for a common end in a situation of interdependence.

This dovetails nicely with research on the theory of constraints (TOC) that comes from the organizational science literature (Goldratt, 1990, 1997; Goldratt & Cox, 1992; Rahman, 1998). Collaborative leadership focused on addressing constraints is one way to move toward retrofitting collaboration into the NPM. The constraints methodology identifies the most important limiting factor or constraint that stands in the way of achieving a goal and then systematically works to improve that constraint until it is no longer the limiting factor. Its proponents portray TOC as a highly focused methodology for creating rapid improvement in organizational performance and service delivery by prioritizing improvement activities iteratively, focusing on the number one constraint.

New Zealand has successfully demonstrated collaborative leadership coupled with a constraints approach in emergency situations. The following example illustrates its potential use in the future. After the earthquakes Christchurch experienced in 2010 and 2011, the entire central business district needed to be closed off because of unsafe buildings and debris on the streets. A priority for the city to begin functioning again was making the streets passable and safe by deciding which buildings had to be demolished and removing the huge mountains of debris the demolition would create. There could have been much interagency wrangling and haggling over who had jurisdiction, who had capability, who had the means, and who had the know-how. That was not the case, however.

Officials from the earthquake response agency, the Christchurch City Council and the Regional Council, all with some of the necessary authority, capability, and knowledge, deliberately and thoughtfully collaborated to get the job done. Their task was deemed urgent because no other recovery activities could begin until this job was done. These were officials with ongoing responsibilities for the city's functioning who all had knowledge of the legacy of problems created by past quick fixes. They knew that they would need to make compromises concerning speed, quality, and appropriate treatment of debris – some of it potentially reusable and therefore requiring separation and storage, some of it toxic materials requiring special treatment.

They tackled the job collaboratively and incrementally, one piece at a time, first determining broad steps, then working from the outside in, gradually reducing the size of the dangerous "no-go zones." They accepted that some of the things they did would not be ideal or best practice through the lens of traditional NPM because of time and resource constraints. For instance, rather than clear areas based on piecemeal organizational boundaries, they met each morning to review where they were at and what new risks or challenges had emerged, then reprioritized as needed, using what resources they had among them irrespective of formal jurisdiction, to continue making progress. They set the goal of getting the job done in the minimum time possible while, importantly, not creating problems for future generations. This latter focus on "do not create a large legacy problem for others to fix in the future" acted as a lens for each agency through which trade-offs and risks of working quickly and pragmatically with many unknowns were viewed. This unifying goal allowed the teams led by the three agencies to work efficiently in a high-trust, successful collaborative arrangement.

This type of move from a traditional leadership culture, where individual accountability reigns supreme, to a collaborative culture where leadership is emergent and shared, was facilitated by the exigencies of the earthquake devastation. Unfortunately, it is common to hear people in government lament how quickly the will to collaborate in the immediate aftermath of the earthquakes evaporated and the organization-centric approach returned. We conclude that collaboration is often seen as a second-rate option to be used "if we have to" and then quickly is replaced by standard NPM piecemeal policy and implementation processes when the emergency or crisis subsides or the stalled policy is unfrozen.

At the same time, there are increasing numbers of people in senior public sector positions who see the need for increased collaboration to create more-responsive and tailored public services, which suggests that the odds of eventual success are promising for New Zealand as well as other strong NPM governments. Indeed, after the initial collaborations necessary to allow New Zealand to respond to the COVID-19 pandemic, for example, public servants are asking, how can we not go backward this time (as they did after the earthquakes).

6.3 Need to Create Space for Collaborative Processes

Collaboration is known from research often to be costly in terms of time, process, procedures, and sometimes perceptions of power (Mitchell, O'Leary, and Gerard, 2015; Bingham and O'Leary, 2008; Huxham, 2003). Yet those who have studied collaboration and performance have found a positive link between the two. Mitchell et al. (2015), for example, using data from federal government managers and city managers in the United States, as well as NGO leaders around the world, concluded:

> Despite differences among the roles and responsibilities of the [1,874] respondents and among the datasets, we conclude that all three groups of respondents view collaboration as a key management and leadership strategy to improve performance and have generally experienced successful performance outcomes through collaboration. In addition to direct performance outcomes, respondents receive additional benefits from collaboration, such as organizational learning and improved relationships that may contribute to longer-term gains. (Mitchell, O'Leary and Gerard, 2015: 710)

Those leading and governing collaborative projects in strong NPM governments have a primary role to play in creating space for collaboration that allows both the time necessary to focus on shared interests, as well as the collaborative capital necessary to achieve joint goals using the knowledge and resources of those involved. We saw in the CWMS and LAWF analyses in Section 5 that considerable time was needed to build a shared understanding of the problem and work out possible ways forward. New capabilities are required of public servants in this phase to resist bounding or rigidly specifying the problem or its solution so tightly as to stifle collaboration and innovation.

Contrasted to this, we saw in Section 3 early trials in supporting at-risk youth, involving central and local government and community organizations that were controlled and overprescribed by the NPM center (that controlled the funding and the accountability processes) limited the program's success. Hence, there is also a need to build an authorizing environment that will value collaborative processes and small steps. Unfortunately, collaboration has been more of a last resort in New Zealand when previous efforts have failed, rather than an alternative way to build solutions that last.

6.4 Need to Cultivate the Collaborative Mindset

Collaboration is deeply dependent on the skills of officials and managers. Important is who is representing an organization, agency, or jurisdiction at the table, whether they can see collaborative advantage, and whether they have the necessary skills to be an effective collaborator (O'Leary and Vij, 2012). Eppel and colleagues found many participants to collaborative efforts just "smiling and nodding ... but not following through on commitments" (2008: 33). Of the 100 individuals O'Leary (2014: 35) interviewed for her study, most agreed that collaboration is essential, but when pressed, most questioned whether they really know how to do it. For example, a South Island local government official said that "people think collaboration is hard, largely because we don't really know how to do it." A New Zealand local government consultant said that "there is an ignorance of how to make large-scale change happen." Another local government consultant said that there is "not much experience among local governments in working with the not-for-profit sector." At a conference of local government officials in Canterbury at which the authors of this Element spoke, one participant turned to the audience and said, "Let's see a show of hands. How many of us in this room have received training in how to collaborate?" Four out of thirty-three participants raised their hand. This, of course, is not solely a New Zealand problem, but demonstrates an additional impediment to collaboration in NPM regimes that continues today: lack of knowledge concerning what collaboration is and how to do it.

In 2012, O'Leary, Choi, and Gerard surveyed 304 members of the US Senior Executive Service (SES) and asked them the question, "What is the skill set of the successful collaborator?" In addition to strategy and technical knowledge (considered baseline or entry-level skills by respondents), the most frequently mentioned answers to the question dealt with personal attributes and interpersonal skills, followed by group process skills.

The most frequently mentioned personal attributes were (in order) openminded, patient, change-oriented, flexible, unselfish, persistent, diplomatic, honest, trustworthy, respectful, empathetic, goal-oriented, decisive, friendly, and a sense of humor. The most frequently mentioned interpersonal skills were good communication, listening, and the ability to work with people.

Tied with this were group process skills, mentioned third in importance as part of the skill set of the successful collaborator. These included facilitation; interest-based negotiation; collaborative problem solving; skill in understanding group dynamics, culture, and personalities; compromise; conflict resolution; and mediation. Taken as a whole, O'Leary, Choi, and Gerard call this "the collaborative mindset."

The collaborative mindset can be acquired by most, and collaborative problem-solving can be learned. Public managers in high-NPM countries would benefit from training in collaboration as a management and leadership strategy, including the essential skills of the collaborative manager. Today, collaboration is part of the skill set expected of New Zealand central government managers, as articulated by SSC, but the challenges of inculcating knowledge and an appreciation of collaboration remain in an NPM culture that still emphasizes the supremacy of the individual organization and its performance and accountabilities over collective outcomes.

6.5 Need for Flexibility and Agility

This Element was written at a time when the world was in the throes of a response to the COVID-19 pandemic. What we saw in New Zealand during this horrific public health emergency was a great deal of flexibility and the ability to move quickly, particularly in the public sector (Lips and Eppel 2021). In fact, New Zealand led the world with its innovative approach, which involved working across agencies and collaborating with community experts. Like the Christchurch earthquake example, collaborative innovation was triggered by crisis.

New Zealand public sector managers have become fond of the term "agile" to refer to reimaging services delivered expeditiously by reprioritizing resources and working with others to achieve something that is needed here and now that can be iteratively refined based on feedback from users over time (Mergel, Ganapati, and Whitford, 2021). This kind of agility is less visible in more usual times, but that doesn't mean it cannot be infused into the system. What is needed is more user-designed and -led, flexible practices by public servants, especially in the way projects or services are designed and delivered. Instead of a set of rigid, predesigned NPM rules and regulations at the outset, which then flow through to implementation, a more flexible collaborative and incremental approach is needed. This means designing and rolling out small steps forward and then evaluating their effect before designing the next step, involving the public often.

Another current example concerns the New Zealand Accident Compensation Corporation (ACC), which is redeveloping its interface with businesses. All businesses must pay ACC levies for their employees as part of the functioning of New Zealand's no-fault insurance called the Accident Compensation Scheme, under which those injured anywhere are assisted with obtaining what they need to recover and return to work. The person injured also receives a replacement for their income if they are unable to work while recovering. The business levy is adjusted according to the risk profile of the business and their track record. Efforts by a business to improve its safety record might result in lower levies.

ACC might support investment that is known to, or likely to, lower the occurrence and severity of injuries (such as the wearing of helmets in forestry work or working with motorcycle riders to teach them safe rules of the road to reduce accidents). A newly created digital interface is designed to make communication between ACC and organizations more efficient, timely, and tailored to the business. The way this is done is through continuous incremental improvements and refinements to a basic web platform based on feedback from users who are included in the design, implementation, and improvement cycles (Eppel and Lips 2021). This is a collaborative, flexible, and agile model for the future.

6.6 Need for Champions, Guardians, and Complexity Translators

In their study of joined-up government and the emergence of collaboration below the radar in New Zealand, Eppel et al. noted the importance of public officials' commitment to obtaining a positive outcome for their clients (Eppel et al., 2008; 2013). To do this, they required three things. First, they needed to understand the problem, necessity, or impediment from the client's perspective. Often this involved an "ah-ha" moment in which public servants were bought face-to-face with a mismatch between the standard services they offered and what was necessary. Second, they needed to recognize that they or their department alone could not solve the problem. They had to then convince other officials who had the resources to work with them. Third, they often worked clandestinely under the radar, not asking permission but using the detailed knowledge they had, not following standard operating procedure, working around the rules. These were experienced public servants with the knowledge and judgment necessary to inform nonstandard practices and they often told the researchers "no one ever got sacked for doing the right thing." Their approach often included obtaining tacit "permission" or encouragement, troubleshooting and protection from a senior manager in the authorizing environment in which they worked. These people whom Eppel et al. called "guardian angels" helped ensure that blockages were removed and potential booby traps were defused by keeping senior managers and politicians informed as needed. Eppel and Lips (2016) consider these public servants "complexity translators." They understand the complexities of the carefully balanced compromises and commitments on the ground and translate these for the organization and the politicians in ways that build confidence in the collaborative to obtain results even when its processes seem indirect or slow.

6.7 Need for Enhanced Functional Leadership and Stewardship

In the early days of NPM in New Zealand in the 1990s, much was made of the freedom managers had to decide what they needed in order to deliver their outputs within the funds allocated by government. Each government department was free to hire the mix of staff it needed and to set market pay rates, for example. This sometimes meant that there was competition among departments for the best staff and salaries. In addition, each department negotiated its own office requirements with agreements sometimes ending up on the front page of newspapers, criticized for an inappropriate use of taxpayer money. Over time, those in charge of the system (Ministers, the State Services Commissioner, and the Treasury) became more sensitive to the inconsistencies, inefficiencies, and conflicts as well as the myriad clashing public sector values this served. Beginning around 2000, there have been numerous changes to the freedoms of chief executives, with the goal of creating greater efficiencies and consistency across the whole of government. For example, negotiation for procurement of property and vehicles is again done centrally by one agency on behalf of the whole public sector.

The ideas of functional leadership and stewardship were introduced into the State Sector Act of 1988 through amendments passed in 2013, thereby altering some of the original NPM propositions. Functional leadership is about one chief executive having responsibility for leading an area across the whole of the state sector, such as digital government or property procurement. Stewardship is about leaders taking into account the longer-term capability and requirements not only of their departments but for the whole of government and New Zealand's future. To accomplish these goals, accounting periods for planning and reporting by departments have been moved from their original one-year duration (where all unused funds were returned to the Crown each year if not spent) to a rolling four-year plan, which allows some flexibility for multiyear programs, and shifts funding into future years if projects do not proceed as expected. These are examples of successful tinkering with NPM to enable collaboration. There is a need for more of this if high-NPM countries are to be able to retrofit collaboration into their regimes.

6.8 Need to Work in Partnership with Other Sectors and with the Public

The "perfect and rational" solution can be the enemy of the "possible," "good enough," and "achievable" solution that can be made better over time. The ACC example of quickly developing the minimum viable product to address a service "pain point," then improving the product based on feedback from users is an illustration of this. So too are the case studies in this Element (CWMS, LAWF, Southern Initiative, and Whānau Ora) where we saw that the solution that works is what those closest to the action think will work best, not what has been designed by others and imposed as an optimal solution.

In Whānau Ora today, government-funded services in Māori communities, codesigned with those communities using local understanding of needs and contexts, are beginning to show results that have previously eluded the government agencies. So too, during New Zealand's COVID-19 response, the use of expertise from outside the government in collaborative partnerships has yielded improvements in the public health agency's capability to track, trace, rapidly identify, and isolate new cases of COVID-19 infection. Epidemiologists and public health specialists from the academic and practitioner sectors have made major contributions to setting public health goals for the government and then analyzing the capability of the public sector to deliver. There is a need for enhanced partnerships with other sectors and with the public in high-NPM countries if the benefits of collaboration are to be realized.

6.9 Important Choices Ahead for New Zealand and Other Strong NPM Countries

By 2019, public sector leaders had reached the conclusion that more than "tinkering" was needed to retrofit collaboration into New Zealand's NPM model. A 2019 review of the New Zealand public service model agreed with many of the conclusions of our research that undergirds this Element, specifically that while much good came from NPM changes in terms of efficiency, a siloed culture that hindered collaboration was an unfortunate by-product. Specifically, it was found that the NPM system had narrowed each department's focus to its own particular outputs, incentivizing officials to focus on their own agency rather than encouraging wider outcomes and a unified, collaborative public service identity. The head of the Public Service in New Zealand referred to public servants needing to have "a spirit of service" (Hughes, 2019: 4). The review concluded that a "collaborative and cohesive public service is necessary in order to address complex issues that span agency boundaries and to provide wrap around services based on New Zealanders' needs, rather than agency convenience" (Public Service Legislation Bill, 2019: 1–2).

Intended to address these issues, the New Zealand Public Service Act of 2020 replaced the State Sector Act of 1988. Viewing the new Act through the lens of collaboration theory and practice presented in this Element, we see several positive steps forward toward retrofitting collaborating into NPM. First, the 1988 Act lacked consideration of how the public sector worked as a whole for citizens. Instead, it treated each individual department as a distinct entity and employer, carrying out the directives of the government of the day, thus opening the potential for gaps in public services as well as competing priorities set by individual ministers that might undermine overall objectives. The new 2020 Act establishes shared purpose, principles, and values for the New Zealand public service and the people working in it. It provides for new organizational forms and ways of working, including "across public service agencies, to achieve better outcomes for the public" (Public Service Act 2020: s3). It also widens the set of public organizations to which the Act applies to include some frontline delivery agencies controlled by their own decision-making boards, such as public schools. It affirms the fundamental goal of government as acting with a spirit of service to the community.

Further, the Act allows for the creation of new types of entities such as cross-sector executive boards, and new departmental agencies with a particular focus on joint ventures to achieve goals that cross several organizations. The stated purpose of interdepartmental executive boards is:

- To align and coordinate strategic policy, planning, and budgeting activities for two or more departments with responsibilities in a subject matter area;
- To support those departments to undertake priority work in the subject matter area; and
- To support cross-department initiatives in the subject matter area. (Public Service Act 2020: s25)

While similar boards have previously existed (such as the one described in the justice sector case in Section 4), the Act encourages their use in the future by giving them formal legal status.

The Act also empowers "interdepartmental ventures that will allow resources to be brought together into a single distinct [collaborative] entity that will be able to hold assets, employ staff, enter into contracts, and administer appropriations just as a public service department does" (Public Service Legislation Explanatory note, 2019: 3). Each joint venture is given official recognition through an order in council, and joint operational agreements specified in the Act create a "formal structure for co-operative and collaborative working arrangements between public service agencies" (Public Service Act 2020: s38). Further, the Act facilitates the staffing of such entities by making it easier for public servants in any one public service agency to be deployed into another department or joint venture with no impediments to their pay or employment conditions. Employer rights, duties, and powers equivalent to those of chief executives are given to these joint ventures, department agencies, and executive boards, a signal that they are intended to be true catalysts of collaboration. The features of the Act identified thus far make us optimistic for a way forward to retrofit collaboration into strong NPM regimes.

The head of the public service (the Public Service Commissioner) is required to establish a public sector leadership team made up of all the public service chief executives and others from the various agencies and boards to both contribute to an effective and cohesive public service, and to work together cooperatively and model leadership behaviors. This part of the legislation makes us hopeful that collaboration might someday move beyond retrofitting, becoming more normalized and supported. The Act continues the focus of the 2013 amendments to the State Sector Act on Leadership on some functions across the public sector (for example, the Chief Digital Officer to lead digital government initiatives across all government agencies), another provision seeking to make collaboration more prevalent.

Active promotion of "stewardship" is enshrined as a principle of public service in the Act, defined as active promotion of the long-term capability, the systems and processes, assets, and the legislation administered by agencies. This is one of the five principles chief executives are charged with upholding, along with political neutrality, free and frank advice, merit-based appointments, and fostering a culture of open government (Public Service Act, 2020: s12). The Act maintains that the "fundamental characteristic of the public service is acting with a spirit of service to the community." Public service leaders, interdepartmental executive boards, boards of interdepartmental ventures, and boards of Crown agents must preserve, protect, and nurture the spirit of service to the community that public service employees bring to their work.

The Act specifies five "public service values" (s14) sought in the work of the public sector:

Impartial – to treat all people fairly, without favor or bias;

Accountable – to take responsibility for its work, actions, and decisions;

Ethical – to act with integrity and be open and transparent;

Respectful – to treat all people with dignity and compassion and act with humility; and

Responsive – to understand and meet people's needs and aspirations.

These values are to be operationalized through codes of conduct to be developed by the Public Service Commissioner.

Examining the way that the provisions of the Act concerning how new collaborative approaches, organizations, and values are created and sustained – through the lens of this Element – gives us pause. These are bureaucratic, centralized, and prescriptive pronouncements articulated in excruciating NPM-like detail in the new legislation. For example, the mandate for a functional chief executive micromanages what must go into such a proposal as follows:

(a) [S]tate the designation of the functional chief executive role; and

(b) identify the department that will be the host department for the role; and

(c) set out the particular functions of the role to be carried out within the host department; and

(d) when establishing a functional chief executive role for the first time, delete the words immediately below the table in Schedule 5.

(5) If a functional chief executive role is established, the Commissioner must appoint a person to that role (s51(4)).

This is one of dozens of instances of an apparent overbureaucratization of mandates intended to catalyze collaboration. Therefore, our hopefulness, optimism, and confidence for what the legislation will enable must be tempered. It is too early for results to be seen in practice. We conclude that the new Public Service Act has laid some foundations that might support more collaboration when needed, but it does not go far enough, and its helpful aspects might be obstructed by bureaucratic central government controls.

The test will come in supporting processes such as the revision of the Public Service Leadership Capability Development Profile, which is a document to guide the practice and professional development of public servants and their leadership skills. There is no reference in the legislation to cultivating the collaborative mindset. There is no hint of an understanding of the need for champions, guardians, and complexity translators within the rank-and-file public servants to make collaboration work. Instead, there are descriptions of boards of high-level executives and managers charged with driving collaboration.

Moreover, there is little encouragement of flexibility and agility, but instead pages of minute, detailed bureaucratic instructions about how to appoint public servants and how new "collaborative" organizations should be created. For example, the detail provided for the duties of chief executives is at once very NPM-like in its focus on efficiency, individual and organizational accountability, and an absence of any duty to support collaborative approaches. See Table 3.

Table 3 An Example of collaborative intent being smothered by new NPM-like mandates in the Public Service Act of 2020

A chief executive of a department or departmental agency is responsible to the appropriate Minister for:

(1) (a) improving ways of working across public service agencies; and (b) their agency's responsiveness on matters relating to the collective interests of government; and (c) the operation of their agency, including in carrying out the purpose of the public service under section 11; and (d) supporting that Minister to act as a good steward of the public interest, including by – (i) maintaining public institutions, assets, and liabilities; and (ii) maintaining the currency of any legislation administered by their agency; and (iii) providing advice on the long-term implications of policies; and (e) the performance of the functions and duties and the exercise of the powers of the chief executive or of their agency (whether those functions, duties, or powers are imposed or conferred by an enactment or by the policies of the Government); and (f) giving advice to Ministers; and (g) the integrity and conduct of the employees for whom the chief executive is responsible; and (h) the efficient and economical delivery of the goods or services provided by the agency and how effectively those goods or services contribute to the intended outcomes.

(2) The chief executive of a department is not responsible for the performance of functions or duties, or the exercise of powers, of or by that part of the department that is a departmental agency hosted by the department unless expressly provided in this Act or another enactment.

(3) The chief executive of a departmental agency is responsible for the performance of functions and duties, and the exercise of powers, by that part of the department that is the departmental agency only and not any functions, duties, or powers of the host department unless expressly provided in this Act or another enactment.

(4) The chief executive of a servicing department of an interdepartmental executive board is not responsible for the performance of functions or duties, or the exercise of powers, of or by the board unless provided in an enactment or delegated to the department under section 27.

(5) However, if the chief executive of a servicing department is also a member of the board they also have full responsibilities as a member of the board.

(Public Sector Act 2020: s52)

One must ask, has New Zealand legislated collaboration to death? Will so many centralized rules and regulations have to be followed to allow collaboration that the creativity that comes from bottom-up collaboration will be stunted? Moreover, the Act strengthens the powers of the Public Service

Commissioner in ways that hearken to the old great man theories of leadership: immense power is given to one person who has the sole authority in many instances to enable or kill collaboration.

As of the writing of this Element, it is too soon to know the effect of this legislative change. The possible tensions and abrasion points for future collaborations, however, are obvious. On the one hand, the legislation makes clear that the public servant's role is to "do the right thing" on behalf of the whole of New Zealand, and that collaboration under certain circumstances will be considered (Scott and Macaulay, 2020). On the other hand, the Act also threatens to impose more rigidity through the codes, rules, and regulations that might just become another straitjacket, producing the same kind of inflexibility in the face of individual needs and circumstances experienced under NPM.

New Zealand's challenges, as with all countries, are not getting any easier. Global climate change, immigration, pollution problems, housing, child poverty, public health, disaster response, and crime are only a few of the examples of cross-boundary challenges that could benefit from collaborative approaches. New Zealand has taken positive steps in recent years to encourage collaboration across boundaries. Attempts at crosscutting initiatives are growing in frequency. Many local and regional governments in New Zealand are doing significant work in the area of collaboration. There is creative collaboration both with and among the public, and among government entities. But more is needed.

Collaboration is hard, and it is not always wise. There is no magic formula or magic elixir that can be used to solve all public problems collaboratively, and there will always be tensions between the tidy, organization-centric NPM approaches and the messiness that sometimes comes with collaboration to solve cross-boundary problems. Retrofitting collaboration into New Zealand and in other strong NPM countries does not mean tossing out all the good that came from the NPM reforms. Rather it means building on these reforms to better serve the public in those areas that can benefit by crossing boundaries.

The examples in this Element demonstrate that working collaboratively across boundaries, with other sectors, and with the public can be done successfully in strong NPM countries. The paradox is that sufficient political will in the form of mandates to collaborate are needed. These must come with an understanding of what it means to collaborate (especially in the areas of leadership and control) when retrofitting collaborative ideas and approaches into the management and accountability culture of strong NPM governments. Collaboration needs to be "baked" into government's administrative systems just as the NPM was "burned" into them decades ago. There are many ways this can be accomplished, including creating alternative institutions for funding public services, their design, delivery, monitoring, and accountability; changing performance indicators to include public values beyond efficiency; and incentivizing and rewarding collaboration by embedding it in performance evaluations and core competencies.

Challenges to data sharing and incompatible technologies that block inter- and intra-agency collaborative work need to be tackled. Structural barriers to interagency work, such as accounting and budgeting roadblocks, need to be changed. Strong NPM governments need to provide enabling environments to buffer short-term factors that undermine success.

Public servants need to be educated about how to work collaboratively, particularly how to do collaboration. This means training in negotiation, facilitation, collaborative problem solving, and conflict management, as well as encouraging the collaborative mindset. They also need to be allowed to carve out time to stretch their ideas and approaches across government and nongovernment boundaries when needed to get the job done. Collaboration champions, guardians, and complexity translators need to be acknowledged and rewarded. Encouraging flexibility and agility, as well as collaborative leadership would also be giant steps forward. Most importantly, those affected by government programs – the public – need to be consulted in the design and implementation phases of all new endeavors.

As the evidence from New Zealand analyzed in this Element shows, there is a compelling case that the time is right to commit to change in high-NPM governments to enable collaborative approaches. The world is growing more complex. Collaboration across boundaries is needed to address societies' most pressing public policy problems and better serve the public, now and in the future.

References

Agranoff, R. and McGuire, M. (2001). Big Questions in Public Network Management Research. *Journal of Public Administration Research and Theory*, 11(3): pp. 295–326.

Agranoff, R. and McGuire, M. (2003a). *Collaborative Public Management: New Strategies for Local Governments*. Washington, DC: Georgetown University Press.

Agranoff, R. and McGuire, M. (2003b). Inside the Matrix: Integrating the Paradigms of Intergovernmental and Network Management. *International Journal of Public Administration*, 26(12), pp. 1401–1422.

Aldrich, H. E. (1979). *Organizations and Environments*. Englewood Cliffs, NJ: Prentice- Hall.

Allen, B., Eppel, E., and Allen, B. (2019). Holding on Tight – NPM and the New Zealand Performance Improvement Framework. *Australian Journal of Public Administration*. https://doi.org/10.1111/1467-8500.12405.

Alter, C. and Hage, J. (1993). *Organizations Working Together*. Newbury Park, CA: Sage.

Andrews, R. (2010). NPM and the Search for Efficiency. In T. Christensen and P. Lægreid, eds., *The Ashgate Research Companion in New Public Management*. Surrey: Ashgate Publishing Limited, pp. 281–294.

Ansell, C. and Gash, A. (2008). Collaborative Governance in Theory and Practice. *Journal of Public Administration Research and Theory*, 18(4), pp. 543–571.

Aucoin, P. (1990). Administrative Reform in Public Management: Paradigms, Principles, Paradoxes and Pendulums. *Governance: An International Journal of Policy, Administration, and Institutions*, 3(2), pp. 115–137.

Aucoin, P. (2010). The Political-Administrative Design of NPM. In T. Christensen and P. Lægreid, eds., *The Ashgate Research Companion in New Public Management*. Surrey: Ashgate Publishing Limited, pp. 33–46.

Bardach, E. (1998). *Getting Agencies to Work Together: The Practice and Theory of Managerial Craftmanship*. Washington, DC: Brookings Institution.

Berry, C., Krutz, G. S., Langner, B. E., and Budetti, P. (2008). Jump-Starting Collaboration: the ABCD Initiative and the Provision of Child Development Services through Medicaid and Collaborators. *Public Administration Review*, 68(3), pp. 480–490.

Bingham, L. B., Nabatchi, T., and O'Leary, R., (2005). The New Governance: Practices and Processes for Stakeholder and Citizen Participation in the Work of Government. *Public Administration Review*, 65(5), pp. 547–558.

Bingham, L. B. and O'Leary, R. (2006). Conclusion: Parallel Play, Not Collaboration: Missing Questions, Missing Connections. *Public Administration Review*, 66, pp. 161–167.

Bingham, L. B. and O'Leary, R., eds. (2008). *Big Ideas in Collaborative Public Management*. New York: ME Sharpe, Inc.

Bisley, A. (2010). *The Land and Water Forum: Making Progress.* Paper presented at the EDS Conference.

Bisley, A. (2013). Speech to the Bluegreen Conference, Tatum Park, March 9. www.landandwater.org.nz/Site/Resources.aspx.

Boston, J. (2010). Basic NPM Ideas and Their Development. In T. Christensen and P. Lægreid, eds., *The Ashgate Research Companion in New Public Management*. Surrey: Ashgate Publishing Limited, pp. 17–32.

Boston, J. (2012). The Eighties: A Retrospective View. Speech accessed January 15, 2020 from www.ipanz.org.nz/Event?Action=View&Event_id=71

Boston, J. (2016). Anticipatory Governance: How Well Is New Zealand Safeguarding the Future? *Policy Quarterly*, 12(3), pp. 11–24.

Boston, J. and Eichbaum, C. (2007). State Sector Reform and Renewal in New Zealand: Lessons for Governance. In G. E. Caiden and T. T. Sup., eds., *The Repositioning of Public Governance: Global Experiences and Challenges*. Taipei: Taiwan National University, pp. 127–179.

Boston, J., Martin, J., Pallot, J., and Walsh, P. (1991). Reshaping the State: New Zealand's Bureaucratic Revolution. *Victoria University of Wellington Print*.

Boston, J., Martin, J., Pallot, J., and Walsh, P. (1996). *Public Management: The New Zealand Model*. Auckland: Oxford University Press.

Bouckaert, G. and Halligan, J. (2008). Comparing Performance across Public Sectors. *Performance Information in the Public Sector*. London: Palgrave Macmillan, pp. 72–93.

Boulton, A. (2019). Whānau Ora: A Culturally-Informed, Social Policy Innovation. *New Zealand Sociology*, 34(2), pp. 23–48.

Boulton, A., Cumming, J., Moore, C., and Smith, V. (2019). Whānau Ora: Indigenous Policy Success Story. In J. Luetjens, M. Mintrom, and P. t'Hart, eds., *Successful Policy Lessons from Australia and New Zealand*. Canberra: ANU Press, pp. 505–529.

Brunsson, N. (2010). New Public Organizations: A Revivalist Movement. In T. Christensen and P. Lægreid, eds., *The Ashgate Research Companion in New Public Management*. Surrey: Ashgate Publishing Limited, pp. 65–82.

Bryson, J. M., Crosby, B. C., and Stone, M. M. (2006). The Design and Implementation of Cross-Sector Collaborations: Propositions from the Literature. *Public Administration Review*, 66, pp. 44–55.

Bryson, J. M., Crosby, B. C., and Stone, M. M. (2015). Designing and Implementing Cross- Sector Collaborations: Needed and Challenging. *Public Administration Review*, 75(5), pp. 647–663.

Burkett, I. (2017). *The Southern Initiative: Reviewing Strengths & Opportunities*. TACSI, The Australian Centre for Social Innovation.

Butterworth, G. V. and Butterworth, S. (1998). *Reforming Education: The New Zealand Experience, 1984–1996*. Palmerston North: Dunmore Press.

Byrkjeflot, H. (2010). Healthcare States and Medical Professions: The Challenges from NPM. In T. Christensen and P. Lægreid, eds., *The Ashgate Research Companion in New Public Management*. Surrey: Ashgate Publishing Limited, pp. 147–160.

Cheung, A. B. L. (2010). NPM in Asian Countries. In T. Christensen and P. Lægreid, eds., *The Ashgate Research Companion in New Public Management*. Surrey: Ashgate Publishing Limited, pp. 131–146.

Chiarello, E. (2015). The War on Drugs Comes to the Pharmacy Counter: Frontline Work in the Shadow of Discrepant Institutional Logics. *Law & Social Inquiry*, 40(1), pp. 82–122.

Choi, I. and Moynihan, D. (2019). How to Foster Collaborative Performance Management? Key Factors in the US Federal Agencies. *Public Management Review*, pp. 1–22.

Christensen, T. and Lægreid, P. (2001). *New Public Management: The Transformation of Ideas and Practice*. Aldershot: Ashgate.

Christensen, T. and Lægreid, P. (2010a). *The Ashgate Research Companion in New Public Management*. Surrey: Ashgate Publishing Limited.

Christensen, T. and Lægreid, P. (2010b). Beyond NPM? Some Development Features. In Christensen T. and P. Lægreid, eds., *The Ashgate Research Companion in New Public Management*. Surrey: Ashgate Publishing Limited, pp. 391–404.

Christensen, T. and Lægreid, P. (2011). Complexity and Hybrid Public Administration – Theoretical and Empirical Challenges. *Public Organization Review*, 11(4), pp. 407–423.

Christensen T. and Lægreid, P. (2012). Governance and Administrative Reforms. In D. Levi-Faur, ed., *The Oxford Handbook of Governance*. Oxford: Oxford University Press, pp. 255–267.

Christensen, T. and Lægreid, P. (2015). Performance and Accountability – A Theoretical Discussion and an Empirical Assessment. *Public Organization Review*, 15(2), pp.207–225.

Connelly, D., Faerman, S., and Zhang, J. (2008). The Paradoxical Nature of Collaboration. In L. B. Bingham and R. O'Leary, eds., *Big Ideas in*

Collaborative Public Management, New York: ME Sharpe, Inc., pp. 17–35.

Controller and Auditor General. (2015). *Whānau Ora: The First Four Years*. Wellington: Office of the Auditor General.

Cosgrave, R., Bishop, F., and Bennie, N. (2003). *Attendance and Absence in New Zealand Schools*. Ministry of Education, Research Division.

Crosby, B. and Bryson, J. (1992; 2005). *Leadership for the Common Good*. San Francisco: Jossey-Bass.

Diefenbach, T. (2009). New Public Management in Public Sector Organizations: The Dark Sides of Managerialistic "Enlightenment." *Public Administration*, 87(4), pp. 892–909.

Dingfelder, J. (2017). *Wicked Water Problems: Can Network Governance Deliver? Integrated Water Management Case Studies from New Zealand and Oregon, USA*. Portland, OR: Portland State University.

Dormer, R. (2014). Whānau Ora and the Collaborative Turn. *International Journal of Public Administration*, 27(12), pp. 835–845.

Dorrell, S. (1993). Public Sector Change is a World-Wide Movement. Speech by the Financial Secretary to the Treasury, Stephen Dorrell, to the Chartered Institute of Public Finance and Accountancy. London, September 23.

Drath, W. H., McCauley, C. D., Palus, C. J., et al. (2008). Direction, Alignment, Commitment: Toward a More Interactive Ontology of Leadership. *The Leadership Quarterly* 10(6), pp. 635–563.

Dunleavy, P., Margetts, H., Tinkler, J., and Bastow, S. (2006). *Digital Era Governance: IT Corporations, the State, and E-Government*. Oxford University Press.

Edwards, B. (2013). *Submission on "Improving Our Resource Management System."* Wellington: Fish & Game.

Elliott, O. V. and Salamon, L. M. (2002). *The Tools of Government: A Guide to the New Governance*. Oxford University Press.

Emerson, K., Nabatchi, T., and Balogh, S. (2012). An Integrative Framework for Collaborative Governance. *Journal of Public Administration Research and Theory*, 22(1), pp. 1–29.

Environment Canterbury. (2017). *Canterbury Water Management Strategy Targets Report*.

Eppel, E. (2013). *Collaborative Governance Case Studies: The Land and Water Forum*. Wellington: Institute for Governance and Policy Studies. https://www.wgtn.ac.nz/__data/assets/pdf_file/0011/1286282/WP13-05-Collaborative-governance-case-studies.pdf.

Eppel, E., Gill, D., Lips, A. M. B., and Ryan, B. (2013). The Cross-organization Collaboration Solution? Conditions, Roles and Dynamics in New Zealand, in

J. O'Flynn, D. Blackman and J. Halligan (eds.), *Crossing Boundaries in Public Management and Policy: The International Experience*. Abingdon, UK, pp. 47–63.

Eppel, E. (2015). Canterbury Water Management Strategy: "A Better Way?" *Policy Quarterly*, 11(4), pp. 49–57.

Eppel, E., Gill, D., Lips, M., and Ryan, B. (2008). *Better Connected Services for Kiwis: A Discussion Document for Managers and Front Line Staff on Better Joining up the Horizontal and the Vertical*. Wellington: Institute of Policy Studies, School of Government, Victoria University of Wellington.

Eppel, E., Gill, D., Lips, M., and Ryan, B. (2013). The Cross-Organization Collaboration Solution? Conditions, Roles and Dynamics in New Zealand. In J. O'Flynn, D. Blackman, and J. Halligan, eds., *Crossing Boundaries in Public Management and Policy: The International Experience*. New York: Routledge, pp. 47–63.

Eppel, E. and Lips, M. (2016). Unpacking the Black Box of Successful ICT-Enabled Service Transformation: How to Join up the Vertical, the Horizontal and the Technical. *Public Money and Management*, 36(1), pp. 39–46.

Eppel, E. and Lips, M. (2021). *MyACC for Business: A Successful Digital Government Case Study*. www.wgtn.ac.nz/egovt/research/case-studies.

Eppel, E. and Allen, B. (forthcoming). Social Services Fragmentation. In K. Baehler, ed., *Oxford Handbook on Governance and Management for Social Policy*. Oxford: Oxford University Press.

Fleishman, R. (2009). To Participate or Not to Participate? Incentives and Obstacles for Collaboration. In L. B. Bingham and R. O'Leary eds., *The Collaborative Public Manager*. Washington, DC: Georgetown University Press, pp. 31–52.

Foster, M. K. and Meinhard, A. G. (2002). A Regression Model Explaining Predisposition to Collaborate. *Nonprofit and Voluntary Sector Quarterly*, 31 (4), pp. 549–564.

Galaskiewicz, J. (1985). Interorganizational Relations. *Annual Review of Sociology* (11), pp. 281–304.

Gazley, B. and Brudney, J. L. (2007). The Purpose and (Perils) of Government-Nonprofit Partnership. *Nonprofit and Voluntary Sector Quarterly*, 36(3), pp. 389–415.

Gill, D. ed. (2011). The Iron Cage Recreated: The Performance Management of State Organizations in New Zealand. Wellington: Institute of Policy Studies.

Gill, D., Eppel, E., Lips, M., and Ryan, B. (2007). Managing for Outcomes: The Breakthrough from the Front Line. *Policy Quarterly*, 3(4), pp. 39–43.

Goldsmith, S. and Kettl, D. F. eds. (2009). Unlocking the Power of Networks: Keys to High-Performance Government. Brookings Institution Press.

Goldratt, E. M. (1990). *Theory of Constraints: What Is This Thing Called Theory of Constraints and How Should It Be Implemented.* Great Barrington, MA: North River Press.

Goldratt, E. M. (1997). *Critical Chain.* Great Barrington, MA: North River Press.

Goldratt, E. M., & Cox, J. (1992). *The Goal: A Process of Ongoing Improvement.* (2nd ed.)Great Barrington, MA: North River Press.

Graddy, E. A. and Chen, B. (2006). Influences on the Size and Scope of Networks for Social Service Delivery. *Journal of Public Administration Research and Theory*, 16(40), pp. 522–533.

Graddy, E. A. and Chen, B. (2009). Partner Selection and the Effectiveness of Interorganizational Collaboration. In L. B. Bingham and R. O'Leary, eds., *The Collaborative Public Manager: New Ideas for the Twenty-First Century.* Washington, DC: Georgetown University Press, pp. 53–70.

Gray, B. (1989). *Collaborating: Finding Common Ground for Multiparty Problems.* San Francisco: Jossey-Bass.

Halligan, J. (2010). NPM in Anglo-Saxon Countries. In T. Christensen and P. Lægreid, eds., *The Ashgate Research Companion in New Public Management.* Surrey: Ashgate Publishing Limited, pp. 83–96.

Halligan, J., Sarrico, C. S., and Rhodes, M. L. (2012). On the Road to Performance Governance in the Public Domain? *International Journal of Productivity and Performance Management. 61*(3), pp. 224–234.

Hansen, H. F. (2010). NPM in Scandinavia. In T. Christensen and P. Lægreid, eds., *The Ashgate Research Companion in New Public Management.* Surrey: Ashgate Publishing Limited, pp. 113–130.

Heclo, H. (1978). Issue Networks and the Executive Establishment. In A. King, ed., *The New American Political System.* Washington, DC: American Enterprise Institute, pp. 87–124.

Hicklin, A., O'Toole, Jr., L. J., Meier, K., and Robinson, S. E. (2009). Calming the Storms: Collaborative Public Management, Hurricanes Katrina and Rita, and Disaster Response. In L. Blomgren Bingham and R. O'Leary, eds., *The Collaborative Public Manager: New Ideas for the Twenty-First Century.* Washington, DC: Georgetown University Press, pp. 95–114.

Hood, C. (1991). A Public Management for All Seasons? *Public Administration*, 69(1), pp. 3–19.

Hood, C. (1995). Contemporary Public Management: A New Global Paradigm? *Public policy and Administration*, 10(2), pp. 104–117.

Hood, C. (1996). Exploring Variations in Public Management Reform of the 1980s. In H. Bekke, J. Perry, and T. A. J. Toonen, eds., *Civil Service Systems in Comparative Perspective*. Bloomington, IN: Indiana University Press, pp. 268–287.

Hood, C., & Peters, G. (2004). The Middle Aging of New Public Management: Into the Age of Paradox? *Journal of Public Administration Research and Theory*, 14(3), pp. 267–282.

Howard-Williams, C., Bisley, A., and Taylor, K. (2013). New Approaches to Planning and Decision-Making for Fresh Water: Cooperative Water Management in New Zealand. In Director General UNESCO, ed., *Free Flow:* Researching Water Security Through Cooperation, pp. 178–181.

Hudson, B., Hardy, B., Henwood, M., and Winstow, G. (1999). In Pursuit of Inter-Agency Collaboration in the Public Sector: What Is the Contribution of Theory and Research? *Public Management*, 1(2), pp. 235–260.

Hughes, P. (2019). Public Service Legislation and Public Service Reform. *Policy Quarterly, 14*(4), pp. 3–7. https://doi.org/10.26686/pq.v15i4.5918

Humpage, L. (2017). Does Having an Indigenous Political Party in Government Make a Difference to Social Policy? The Maori Party in New Zealand. *Journal of Social Policy*, 46(3), pp. 475–494.

Huxham, C. (1993). Pursuing Collaborative Advantage. *The Journal of the Operational Research Society*, 44(6), pp. 599–611.

Huxham, C. (2003). Theorizing Collaboration Practice. *Public Management Review*, 5(3), pp. 401–423.

Imperial, M. T. (2005). Using Collaboration as a Governance Strategy: Lessons from Six Watershed Management Programs. *Administration and Society*, 37 (3), pp. 281–320.

Imperial, M. T., Ospina, S., Johnston, E., O'Leary, R., Thomsen, J., Williams, P., and Johnson, S. (2016). Understanding Leadership in a World of Shared Problems: Advancing Network Governance in Large Landscape Conservation. *Frontiers in Ecology and the Environment, 14*(3), pp. 126–134.

Isett, K. R., Mergel, I. A., LeRoux, K., Mischen, A., and Rethemeyer, R. K. (2011). Networks in Public Administration Scholarship: Understanding Where We Are and Where We Need to Go. *Journal of Public Administration Research and Theory, 21* (suppl_1), pp. i157–i173.

Johnston, E. W., Hicks, D., Nan, N. and Auer, J. C. (2011). Managing the Inclusion Process in Collaborative Governance. *Journal of Public Administration Research and Theory, 21*(4), pp. 699–721.

Kettl, D. F. (2000). The Transformation of Governance: Globalization, Devolution, and the Role of Government. *Public Administration Review*, 60 (6), pp. 488–497.

Kettl, D. F. (2006). Managing Boundaries in American Administration: The Collaboration Imperative. *Special issue, Public Administration Review*, 66, pp. 10–19.

Kettl, D. F. (2016). *Politics of the Administrative Process*. Washington, DC: CQ Press.

Kickert, W. J. M. (2010). Public Management Reform in Continental Europe: National Distinctiveness. In T. Christensen and P. Lægreid, eds., *The Ashgate Research Companion in New Public Management*. Surrey: Ashgate Publishing Limited, pp. 97–112.

Kickert, W. J. M., Klijn, E.-H., and Koppenjan, J. F. M., eds. (1997). *Managing Complex Networks: Strategies for the Public Sector*. Sage.

Kingdon, J. W. (2010). *Agendas, Alternatives, and Public Policies*. 2nd ed. New York: Pearson.

Kirk, N. A. (2015). *Local Government Authority and Autonomy in Canterbury's Freshwater Politics Between 1989 and 2010*. Lincoln, NZ: Lincoln University.

Knight, C. (2019). A Potted History of Freshwater Management in New Zealand. *Policy Quarterly*, 15(3), pp. 3–7.

Land and Water Forum. (2010). *Report of the Land and Water Forum: A Fresh Start for Freshwater*. Wellington: Land and Water Forum.

Land and Water Forum. (2012a). *Second Report of the Land and Water Forum: Setting Limits for Water Quality and Quantity a Freshwater Policy- and Plan-Making through Collaboration*. Wellington: Land and Water Forum.

Land and Water Forum. (2012b). *Third Report of the Land and Water Forum: Managing Water Quality and Allocating Water Cover*. Wellington: Land and Water Forum

Land and Water Forum. (2015). *Fourth Report of the Land and Water Forum*. Wellington: Land and Water Forum.

Lane, J. E. (2000). *New Public Management*. London: Routledge.

Levine, S., & White, P. E. (1961). Exchange as a conceptual framework for the study of interorganizational relationships. *Administrative Science Quarterly*, 5(4), 583–601. doi:10.2307/2390622

Lewis, E. (1980). *Public Entrepreneurship: Toward a Theory of Bureaucratic Political Power*. Bloomington: Indiana University Press.

Lips, A. M. B., O'Neil, R. R., and Eppel, E. A. (2011). Cross-Agency Collaboration in New Zealand: An Empirical Study of Information Sharing Practices, Enablers and Barriers in Managing for Shared Social Outcomes. *International Journal of Public Administration* 34(4) pp. 255–266.

Lips, M., and Eppel, E. (2021). Effects of Covid-19 on Digital Public Services. *Chair in Digital Government*, Victoria University of Wellington. www.wgtn

.ac.nz/egovt/news/2020/1921356-effects-of-covid-19-on-digital-public-services.

Lodge, M. , and Gill, D. (2011). Toward a New Era of Administrative Reform? The Myth of Post-NPM in New Zealand. *Governance*, 24(1), pp. 141–166.

Logan, H. (2013). Inside the Black Box: The Influence of Government Executive Forces on Environmental Policy Effectiveness in New Zealand. (PhD doctoral thesis). Lincoln University, New Zealand.

Lorenz, C. (2012). If You're So Smart, Why Are You Under Surveillance? Universities, Neoliberalism, and New Public Management. *Critical Inquiry*, 38 (3), pp. 599–629.

Mandell, M. and Steelman, T. A. (2003). Understanding What Can Be Accomplished through Interorganizational Innovations: The Importance of Typologies, Context and Management Strategies. *Public Management Review*, 5(2), pp. 197–224.

Mayne, J. W. and Zapico-Goii, E., eds. (2017). *Monitoring Performance in the Public Sector: Future Directions from International Experience*. Routledge.

Mergel, I. A., Ganapati, S., & Whitford, A. (2021). Agile: A New Way of Governing. *Public Administration Review*, 81(1), pp. 161–165. https://doi.org/0.1111/puar.13202

McGuire, M. (2009). The New Professionalism and Collaborative Activity in Local Emergency Management. In L. Blomgren-Bingham and R. O'Leary, eds., *The Collaborative Public Manager: New ideas for the Twenty-First Century*. Washington, DC: Georgetown University Press, pp. 71–94.

Ministry for the Environment. (2013). *Freshwater Reform 2013 and Beyond*. Wellington: Ministry for the Environment.

Ministry of Social Development (MSD). (2013). *Social Sector Trials – Trialing New Approaches to Social Sector Change: Final Evaluation Report*. Wellington: Ministry of Social Development.

Mitchell, G. E., O'Leary, R., and Gerard, C. (2015). Collaboration and Performance: Perspectives from Public Managers and NGO Leaders. *Public Performance & Management Review*, 38(4), pp. 684–716.

Mizrahi, S. (2017). *Public Policy and Performance Management in Democratic Systems: Theory and Practice*. Springer.

Morrison, A. (2014). Picking Up the Pace in Public Services. *Policy Quarterly*, May, pp. 43–48.

Moynihan, D. (2008). *The Dynamics of Performance Management: Constructing Information and Reform*. Georgetown University Press.

Nabatchi, T., Gastil, J., Leighninger, M., and Weiksner, G. M. eds. (2012). *Democracy in Motion: Evaluating the Practice and Impact of Deliberative Civic Engagement*. Oxford University Press.

New Zealand Productivity Commission. (2015). *More Effective Social Services*. Wellington: New Zealand Productivity Commission.

New Zealand. (2019). Public Service Legislation Bill. Accessed July 20, 2020 from https://www.legislation.govt.nz/bill/government/2019/0189/latest/d795037e2.html P. 1–2

Norman, E. J. R. (2003). *Obedient Servants?: Management Freedoms and Accountabilities in the New Zealand Public Sector*. Victoria University Press.

O'Leary, R. (2014). *Collaborative Governance in New Zealand: Important Choices Ahead*. Wellington, NZ: Fulbright New Zealand.

O'Leary, R., and Bingham, L. B. (2007). *A Manager's Guide to Resolving Conflicts in Collaborative Networks*. Washington, DC: Center for the Business of Government.

O'Leary, R., Choi, Y., and Gerard, C. M. (2012). The Skill Set of the Successful Collaborator. *Public Administration Review, 72(s1)*, pp. 70–83.

O'Leary, R., Gerard, C., and Bingham, L. B. (2006). Introduction to the Symposium on Collaborative Public Management. *Public Administration Review, 66*, pp. 6–9.

O'Leary, R. and Vij, N. (2012). Collaborative Public Management: Where Have We Been and Where Are We Going? *The American Review of Public Administration*, 42(5), pp. 507–522.

Osborne, D., and Gaebler, T. (1992). Reinventing Government: How the Entrepreneurial Spirit Is Transforming the Public Sector. Reading, MA: Addison Wesley.

Osborne, S. (2010). Delivering Public Services: Time for a New Theory. *Public Management Review, 12*(1), pp. 1–10.

Osborne, S., Radnor, Z., and Nasi, G. (2013). A New Theory for Public Service Management? Toward a (public) Service-Dominant Approach. *The American Review of Public Administration*, 43(2), pp. 135–158.

Ostrom, E. (1990). *Governing the Commons: The Evolution of Institutions for Collective Action*. Cambridge University Press.

Page, S. (2004). Measuring Accountability for Results in Interagency Collaboratives. *Public Administration Review*, 64(5), pp. 591–606.

Pallesen, T. (2010). Privatization. In T. Christensen and P. Lægreid, eds., *The Ashgate Research Companion in New Public Management*. Surrey: Ashgate Publishing Limited, pp. 251–264.

Parliamentary Commissioner for the Environment. (2015). *Managing Water Quality: Examining the 2014 National Policy Statement.* Wellington.

Peters, B. G. (2010). Responses to NPM: From Input Democracy to Output Democracy. In T. Christensen and P. Lægreid, eds., *The Ashgate Research Companion in New Public Management.* Surrey: Ashgate Publishing Limited, pp. 362–374.

Peters, B. G. and Savoie, D. J., eds. (1998). *Taking Stock: Assessing public Sector Reforms.* Canada: Canadian Centre for Management Development.

Pfeffer, J. and Salancik, G. R. (1978). *The External Control of Organizations: A Resource Dependence Perspective.* Stanford, CA: Stanford University Press.

Policy Toolbox (n.d.) https://dpmc.govt.nz/our-programmes/policy-project/policy-methods-toolbox/start-right accessed March 30, 2021.

Pollitt, C. (1990). Performance Indicators: Root and Branch. In M. Cave, M. Kogan, and R. Smith, eds., *Output and Performance Measurement in Government: The State of the Art.* London, Jessica Kingsley: pp. 167–178.

Pollitt, C. (1993). Managerialism and the Public Services: Cuts or Cultural Change in the 1990s? 2nd ed. Oxford: Blackwell.

Pollitt, C. (1993). *Managerialism and the Public Services.* 2nd ed. Hoboken, NJ: Wiley-Blackwell.

Pollitt, C. (1995). Justification by Works or by Faith? Justifying the New Public Management, *Evaluation*, 1(2), pp. 133–154.

Pollitt C. (2002). Clarifying Convergence: Striking Similarities and Durable Differences in Public Management Reform. *Public Management Review*, 4 (1), pp. 471–492.

Pollitt, C. (2003). *The Essential Public Manager.* Buckingham: Open University Press/McGraw Hill.

Pollitt, C. (2016). Managerialism Redux? *Financial Accountability and Management*, 32(4), pp. 429–447.

Pollitt, C. and Bouckaert, G. (2017). *Public Management Reform: A Comparative Analysis – into the Age of Austerity.* 4th ed. Oxford: Oxford University Press.

Public Service Legislation Bill. (2019) P. 1–2. https://www.legislation.govt.nz/bill/government/2019/0189/latest/d795037e2.html

Public Service Act 2020. (2020). https://legislation.govt.nz.

Rahman, S. (1998). Theory of Constraints: A Review of the Philosophy and Its Applications. *International Journal of Operations & Production Management*, 18(4), pp. 336–355.

Rogers, D. L. and Whetten, D. A. (1982). *Interorganizational Coordination: Theory, Research and Implementation*. Ames, IA: Iowa State University Press.

Room, G. (2016). *Agile Actors on Complex Terrains. Transformative Realism and Public Policy*. London: Routledge.

Sabatier, P. (1993). Policy Change over a Decade or More. In H. Jenkins-Smith and P. Sabatier, eds., *Policy Change and Learning: An Advocacy Coalition Approach*. Boulder, CO: Westview Press, pp. 13–40.

Salmon, G. (2008). *Governance of the Rural Environment – Are Existing Approaches Working?* Paper presented at the Conflict in Paradise: The Transformation of Rural New Zealand. Environmental Defence Society Conference. Auckland.

Salmon, G. (2012). *Canterbury Water Management Strategy: A Case Study in Collaborative Governance*. Report prepared for the Ministry for the Environment. Wellington: Ministry for the Environment.

Scott, G. C. (2001). *Public Sector Management in New Zealand: Lessons and Challenges*. Centre for Law and Economics, Australian National University.

Scott, R. J. and Macaulay, M. (2020). Making Sense of New Zealand's "Spirit of Service": Social Identity and the Civil Service. *Public Money & Management*, *40*(8), pp.579–588.

Schick, A. (1996). *The Spirit of the Reform: Managing the New Zealand State Sector in a Time of Change*. Wellington, NZ: State Services Commission and The Treasury. Accessed January 15, 2020 from www.ssc.govt.nz/spirit-of-reform.

Scott, G., Bushnell, P., and Sallee, N. (1990). Reform of the Core Public Sector: New Zealand Experience. *Governance*, 3(2), pp. 138–167.

Scott, R. (2018). *Interagency Collaboration to Reduce Crime. ANZOG Case Study* 2018-198.1.

Smith, V., Moore, C., Cumming, J., and Boulton, A. (2019). In J. Luetjens, M. Mintrom, and P.'t Hart, eds., Whānau Ora: Indigenous Policy Success Story. *Successful Public Policy: Lessons from Australia and New Zealand*, pp. 505–529.

Sowa, J. E. (2008). Implementing Interagency Collaborations: Exploring Variation in Collaborative Ventures in Human Service Organizations. *Administration and Society*, 40(3), pp. 298–323.

Sowa, J. E. (2009). The Collaboration Decision in Nonprofit Organizations: Views from the Front Line. *Nonprofit and Voluntary Sector Quarterly*, 38(6), pp. 1003–1025.

State Services Commission. (2002). *The Review of the Centre – One Year on: Getting Better Results for Citizens, Ministers and Staff.* Wellington, NZ: State Services Commission.

Talbot, C. (2010). *Theories of Performance: Organizational and Service Improvement in the Public Domain.* Oxford University Press.

Taskforce on Whanau-centered Initiatives (TWCI). (2010). *Report of the Taskforce on Whanau-Centered Initiatives.* Wellington: Ministry of Social Development.

The Southern Initiative. (2018). *The Year in Review 2017.* Auckland.

The Southern Initiative. (2019). *The Year in Review 2018.* Auckland.

Thomson, A. M., Perry, J. K., and Miller, T. K. (2008). Linking Collaborative Performance: Aligning Policy Intent, Design, and Impact. In L. Bingham and R. O'Leary, eds., *Big Ideas in Collaborative Public Management.* New York, NY: ME Sharpe, pp. 97–120.

The Treasury. (1984). *Economic Management.* Wellington, NZ: Government Printer.

The Treasury. (1987). *Government Management.* Wellington, NZ: Government Printer.

Tyson, J. (2005). ANZSOG Case Studies: A Voluntary Environmental Accord for the Diary Industry. Parts A and B. In: ANZSOG Case Library www.anzsog.edu.au/resource-library/case-library

Tyson, J. (2014). ANZSOG Case Studies: Responsibility without Regulation: A Dilemma for the Dairy Industry. Parts A and B. In: ANZSOG Case Library www.anzsog.edu.au/resource-library/case-library

Van de Ven, A. H., Emmett, D. C., and Koenig Jr, R. (1975). Frameworks for Interorganizational Analysis. *Interorganizational Theory,* pp. 19–38.

Van Dooren, W. and Van de Walle, S. (2008). Introduction: Using Public Sector Performance Information. *Performance Information in the Public Sector.* London: Palgrave Macmillan, pp. 1–8.

Vangen, S. and Huxham C. (2012). The Tangled Web: Unraveling the Principle of Common Goals in Collaborations. *Journal of Public Administration Research and Theory,* 22(4), pp. 731–760.

Verhoest, K. (2010). The Relevance of Culture for NPM. In T. Christensen and P. Lægreid, eds., *The Ashgate Research Companion in New Public Management. Surrey: Ashgate Publishing Limited,* pp. 47–64.

Vigoda, E. (2002). From Responsiveness to Collaboration: Governance, Citizens, and the Next Generation of Public Administration. *Public Administration Review,* 62(5), pp. 527–540.

Wood, D. J. and Gray, B. (1991). Collaborative Alliances: Moving from Practice to Theory. *The Journal of Applied Behavioral Science*, 23(3), pp. 3–22.

Xialong, T., & Christensen, T. (2019). Beyond NPM to Post NPM? A Study of China's Government Reforms over the Past 40 Years. *American Review of Public Administration*, 49(7), 855–865. doi:10.1177/0275074019849122

Cambridge Elements $^{\equiv}$

Public and Nonprofit Administration

Andrew Whitford
University of Georgia
Andrew Whitford is Alexander M. Crenshaw Professor of Public Policy in the School of Public and International Affairs at the University of Georgia. His research centers on strategy and innovation in public policy and organization studies.

Robert Christensen
Brigham Young University
Robert Christensen is professor and George Romney Research Fellow in the Marriott School at Brigham Young University. His research focuses on prosocial and antisocial behaviors and attitudes in public and nonprofit organizations.

About the Series
The foundation of this series is cutting-edge contributions on emerging topics and definitive reviews of keystone topics in public and nonprofit administration, especially those that lack longer treatment in textbook or other formats. Among keystone topics of interest for scholars and practitioners of public and nonprofit administration, it covers public management, public budgeting and finance, nonprofit studies, and the interstitial space between the public and nonprofit sectors, along with theoretical and methodological contributions, including quantitative, qualitative and mixed-methods pieces.

The Public Management Research Association
The Public Management Research Association improves public governance by advancing research on public organizations, strengthening links among interdisciplinary scholars, and furthering professional and academic opportunities in public management.

Cambridge Elements ☰

Public and Nonprofit Administration

Printed in the United States
by Baker & Taylor Publisher Services